Praise for Laura Lippman

"... special, even extraordinary."
—Stephen King

"She is simply a brilliant novelist."
—Gillian Flynn

"... one of America's most important literary voices."
—*Irish Times*

"[Lippman] seems to only be getting better."
—*Entertainment Weekly*

"A total pro."
—*People*

"She's one of the best novelists around, period."
—*Washington Post*

MY LIFE
AS A
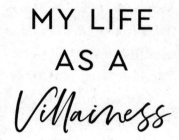

MY LIFE
AS A
Villainess

Essays

LAURA
LIPPMAN

wm

WILLIAM MORROW

An Imprint of HarperCollinsPublishers

Page 271 serves as a continuation of the copyright page.

I have changed the names of some individuals, and modified
identifying features, including physical descriptions and occupations,
of other individuals in order to preserve their anonymity. In
some cases, composite characters have been created or timelines
have been compressed, in order to further preserve privacy and
to maintain narrative flow. The goal in all cases was to protect
people's privacy without damaging the integrity of the story.

HarperCollins books may be purchased for educational, business,
or sales promotional use. For information, please email the
Special Markets Department at SPsales@harpercollins.com.

FIRST EDITION

Designed by Diahann Sturge

Pitchfork art © mStudioVector / Shutterstock, Inc.

Library of Congress Cataloging-in-Publication
Data has been applied for.

ISBN 978-0-06-299733-3

20 21 22 23 24   LSC   10 9 8 7 6 5 4 3 2 1

For the Grotto

Contents

Part III: My Life as a Villainess

Part IV: Genius

"Well, she's not shy."

—Madeline Lippman, numerous times

MY LIFE AS A

AS A

Villainess

Introduction

The Accidental Essayist

Paradox: How does one write about one's distaste for the first-person pronoun without using it? Especially in the introduction to a collection of personal essays?

I give up.

I started my writing life as a newspaper reporter. I am immensely proud of the fact that I supported myself through my writing from the day I left college, more or less. (During the first six months at my first newspaper job, I also worked lunch shifts at the finest Italian restaurant in Waco, Texas.) As a young reporter, I couldn't wait to get my hands on that big shiny "I." But that personal pronoun was the prerogative of columnists, seasoned and proven stylists with distinctive points of view. One had to pay one's dues to write in the first person. I spent twenty years as a reporter, working at four newspapers, and while I slipped a little first-person in here and there, it became less and less desirable to me. Other people's lives were so much more fascinating than mine.

But in 2017, I decided I wanted to challenge myself by writing for a larger variety of publications. And because I was pressed for time and couldn't afford to do the reporting necessary for long-form journalism, I had to mine my personal experiences and small areas of expertise. Initially, I wasn't ready to reveal much about myself, so I kept the canvas small—a piece about my enthusiasm for the writer Ruth McKenney, a "confession" about how I flew to Providence, Rhode Island, for lunch in order to retain A-list status on Southwest Airlines for another year.

Not long after my trip to Providence, I was alone one night as my daughter slept, with only Twitter to keep me company. A subscriber to Longreads—I'm a big believer in paying for content—I stumbled on its section devoted to aging, Fine Lines. It was edited by Sari Botton and because we followed each other on Twitter, I could slide into her DMs, as you kids say, and beg for a chance to write for her. This was tacky and inappropriate, but it worked. She said she would take a piece from me about my status as the Oldest Mom in my peer group.

Five months later, just before Mother's Day, Longreads published my piece, "Game of Crones," and while it didn't go viral, it was immensely popular, quickly stacking up tens of thousands of reads. But the oddest thing was how many women seemed to identify with my description of life as a very old, very unusual working mother. I had thought my experiences were so bizarre that they would function as amusement for "normal" people. Instead, I was reminded that the more specific one is about one's life, the more universal it can seem. I was asked to write more personal essays.

The result is this book, *My Life as a Villainess*. The title is meant to be arch and, I hope, entirely past-tense. I try to be a good person most days, but it does require some effort on my part. Some people think I'm hard on myself in these pages, but I feel that I'm just gleefully honest. In dreams begin responsibilities and I never lose sight of the fact that my dreams have come true. When the William Hurt character asks the Albert Brooks character in *Broadcast News* what to do when reality outstrips one's fantasies, the advice is: "Keep it to yourself." But I just can't.

There is a sense of liberation in admitting to one's faults. I do struggle with being a good friend. If grudge-holding counted for cardio, I'd have run the equivalent of many Boston marathons by now. To me, the joke of this book is how hard I had to stretch to earn the title. "Good girl" is my factory default setting and I had to look hard for evidence of my villainy. It was much easier to talk about aging, my beloved parents, and the various types of geniuses I've been lucky to know.

So when I call myself a beta, a jerk, or worse, it's not self-deprecation; I have spent much of my adult life learning to eschew self-deprecation and encourage other women to do the same. Conversely, when I say nice things about myself, I recognize that's a subversive act for anyone in our humblebrag culture, but especially a middle-aged woman. I do not feel bad about my neck or any other parts of me that are simply succumbing to age. I consider myself a helpful and supportive mentor to many younger writers. And I sincerely believe that the MacArthur Foundation should give me one of its annual grants if only because it's not good for a household with two creative people to have one officially designated as a "genius" when the other is not.

Does a collection of fifteen essays constitute a memoir? Not in this case. There is no mention of my sister, whom I adore, and this omission should thrill her, as she once asked me to promise—in writing—never to produce a memoir. Large swaths of my life are missing—my idyllic childhood in a Brigadoon-like Baltimore neighborhood, Harand Camp of the Theatre Arts, my two-plus decades as a crime novelist, my foodie inclinations, my affection for visionary art, even a couple of near-death experiences. (Falling through the ice while skating, getting into a car driven by a friend zonked on quaaludes and then walking away from the inevitable accident, which has to be the most 1980 story *ever*.)

Is the whole greater than the parts? I think so. I hope so. This is a book about a deeply wonderful life, to quote Laurie Colwin, one of many writers name-checked in these essays. I first started fantasizing about being a novelist when I was twelve and it is everything I hoped for—and more. Again, in dreams begin responsibilities, and as I thunder down the stretch toward official old age, I find I have the confidence and self-esteem to tell the worst stories I know about myself.

The question that hovers over anyone who dares to write personal essays, especially a woman, is, "Who the hell do you think you are?" Before you can answer, you will be told who and what you are not. You are not Nora Ephron. You are not Joan Didion. You are not Susan Sontag. You aren't all that interesting. The list goes on and on; the question is always rhetorical.

I will answer the question anyway. I am: a mother, wife, daughter, sister. I am a writer. I am a person with six decades of life experience under my belt. I am a patriot. I am in therapy. I am silly. I am serious. I am an insomniac. I am a Howard Stern superfan. I'm a grudge-holder. I am a friend, although not a good one. I can be a real asshole. Finally, to steal from my beloved James M. Cain, who once ended a book's introduction with these very words: "I am a registered Democrat. I drink."

Laura Lippman
Baltimore, MD
December 2019

Part I
Game of Crones

I grow old, I grow old, I shall wear my trousers rolled . . . and from Chico's.

The Whole 60

1.

When I was in high school, I would walk to the Waldenbooks in the mall near my home and read novels while standing up. This was the 1970s, long before bookstores became places that encouraged people to sit, hang, browse. There were no armchairs in that narrow store on the second floor of the Mall in Columbia in Howard County, Maryland.

Reading while standing up felt like stealing, a pathetic thrill for this straight-A goody-goody. I had money—I babysat, I eventually worked at the Swiss Colony in the same mall. I could buy any volume I truly desired. But my stand-up reads were books too embarrassing to bring home. I remember only two.

One was *The Greengage Summer* by Rumer Godden, a British novelist perhaps best known today for inspiring the name of Bruce Willis's and Demi Moore's oldest daughter. It now strikes me as a perfectly respectable book; I could have forked over $1.25 for it.

The other one was—I couldn't begin to tell you the title. It was a slick psycho serial killer tale that began with a young couple parked on Lovers Lane, where they were attacked by a man with, if I recall correctly, a metal hook for one of his hands. He used his hook to slash the roof of the convertible, or maybe it was a knife, and as the metal blade (or the hook) pierced through the canvas, the beautiful, vain sorority girl—it was implicit that she deserved to die if only for her smugness—thought: "*I should have had that slice of cheesecake at dinner.*"

It has taken me more than forty years, but the singular achievement of my life may be that if I am attacked by a serial killer on a deserted Lovers Lane, I almost certainly will have had dessert. Not cheesecake, because I don't like cheesecake. Possibly some dark chocolate, preferably with nuts or caramel, or a scoop of Taharka ice cream, an outstanding Baltimore brand, or one of my own home-made blondies, from the SmittenKitchen recipe.

Maybe a shot of tequila, an excellent digestif. Maybe tequila *and* a blondie.

But only if I want those things. Many nights, I'm not in the mood for anything sweet after dinner. Every day, one day at a time, one meal at a time, one hunger pang at a time, I ask myself what I *really* want. I then eat whatever it is.

It is the hardest thing I have ever done in my life.

2.

Every girl remembers her first diet. Usually, it's her mother's.

My mother was (and continues to be, at the age of eighty-eight) slender and fit. As a child, she was part of a group of underweight campers "ordered" to drink daily milkshakes. On her wedding day, she weighed 102 pounds. Why do I recall these facts? I know only that I know them. Her wedding dress hung in the hall closet outside my bedroom, sealed in a plastic bag, but I was never going to wear it. When I was little, that dress—a lovely knee-length shift—was too plain to fit into my future wedding fantasies. And by the time I was ten or eleven, it was clear that I was never going to fit into a dress made for someone who weighed 102 pounds.

In her mid-thirties, my mother gained some weight and decided to go on a diet. This seemed like an adult rite of passage to me, a journey that I would inevitably undertake one day, heading out on the bounding billows of Tab. My mother's diet was a topic of much discussion in our family—and much teasing by my father. My father also was rail-thin; at the age of twelve, I managed to shimmy into his old Navy uniform for the Fourth of July parade. My older sister was thin as well. Many, many, many years later, a good friend saw me with my family at my stepson's bar mitzvah and asked: "Did you get all the nutrients?" This was the first time that anyone had ever suggested there was anything attractive about my size relative to my family's.

In case it's not clear, I was never thin. I am tall, big-boned, with a belly that tends toward protrusion. I was maybe ten or eleven, close to the age my own daughter is now, when my mother cupped her hand over my convex midsection and said, "Look at your little potbelly." Because I was a weird kid who sneaked into the adult side of the library to read adult books—you may sense a theme emerging—I had read Max Shulman's *Barefoot Boy with Cheek*. In that comic college novel, a girl goes to a party where guests are instructed to dress as song titles. She chooses "Smoke Gets in Your Eyes" and wears a gown with a bare midriff, a smudge pot "cunningly hinged" to her navel. This is how I saw my potbelly—a literal pot, a growth, a foreign object hinged, not so cunningly, to my navel.

By the time I was fourteen—fourteen!—I was plotting furiously in my diary: *How To Get a Man*. Step 1, of course, was to get a flat stomach. At the age of fifteen, about the same time I was reading books standing up at the mall, I signed up for a dance class, God knows why. The dance teacher, the mother of a close friend, screamed at me: "LAURA LIPPMAN YOU HAVE A POTBELLY YOU ARE TOO YOUNG TO HAVE A POTBELLY I AM ALLOWED TO HAVE A POTBELLY BUT YOU ARE NOT!"

My first summer home from college I worked as a lifeguard at a small apartment complex where no one knew me, which gave me license to wear a two-piece bathing suit. An older man kept asking me out. After my third or fourth turndown, he guessed my weight almost to the decimal point, then assured me: "If you lost twenty pounds, you would be a knockout."

Then there was the man I loved so much and he loved me, too, until he fell in love with someone else. "It's funny," he mused. "You're not really my type. I like petite women." And off he went with a waif.

Every woman on the planet knows the rest of this story. Diet blah blah blah body dysmorphia yadda yadda yadda Atkins Scarsdale etc. etc., keto, South Beach. We can all write list poems of the eating plans we have undertaken, the measurements over which we obsessed, the various low-carb sects to which we converted. I have nothing new to say about any of this.

What is new is that I have decided, at the age of sixty, that I *am* a goddamn knockout. Like Dorothy at the end of the film version of *The Wizard of Oz*, I had the power I sought all along. I rub my thighs together—sorry, couldn't resist—and tell myself over and over that I am beautiful and, what do you know, suddenly I am. Then I cup my hand over my nine-year-old daughter's gorgeous, solid abdomen and tell her she is beautiful, too.

She's not sure. She asks: "Is there a way to eat that makes a person lose weight?"

No, I tell her. Eat what you want when you want it and your body will figure out what it wants to be. Trust your body.

And then I leave the room and cry a little. I helped to do this. Although I never said the word "diet" in front of my daughter, never spoke about anyone's weight, I did this to her. Kids don't miss a trick and my daughter saw how I used to dress in the morning, how I turned to examine my profile, standing tall, sucking in my gut, smoothing the front of my pants or skirt. She noticed when I stopped eating bread the year she was three. Yes, I tried Whole30 six years ago, and yes, it worked for a while, how could it not? You try not to lose weight while abstaining from alcohol, grains, dairy, and legumes.

Now try deciding what you actually want and tell me which is harder.

3.

Thanks to our modern world, I can pinpoint almost to the minute when I decided to give up dieting. As a former Weight Watchers customer—*of course* I am a former Weight Watchers customer—I received an email when the

company announced it was rebranding itself as WW—
"wellness that works." Suddenly the whole con was clear
to me. On September 24, 2018, at 11:42 A.M., I DM'ed a
screenshot of the email to a friend and added: "fuck it NO
MORE DIETING. EVER."

I continued:

"I have been worried about my weight for forty-five
years, I can't do this anymore. I can't do this to my kid.
I'm almost sixty years old and some part of me is still
worried that not enough men find me fuckable. People
talk about the White House distracting us, nothing has
distracted me as much as this stupid battle with my
weight and my looks, both of which are fine, almost ev-
erybody's weight and face is [sic] fine, and way too many
benefit from getting us to think otherwise.

"What would happen to the global economy if all the
women on the planet suddenly decided: I don't care if
you think I'm fuckable."

I don't know how the global economy is doing, but
this one consumer is trying hard to keep her dollars, her
clicks, and vast swaths of brain real estate from worrying
about whether men desire her.

I appear on a radio show several times a year and

sometimes I say things that men don't like. For example, I once opined that homophobia isn't the only thing
wrong with "jokes" about men raping other men. They're
rape jokes and rape jokes aren't funny.

When I say things like that, there are men who
want to set me straight. "You rape my eyes, you rape
my ears, you rape food," one wrote, beneath a copy of
my perfectly lovely author photo. That's the running
theme: These men do not want to have sex with me. I
joke about this with the radio show's producer, tell him
I have found common ground with my Internet trolls:
They don't want to have sex with me and I don't want to
have sex with them. But who am I kidding?

They *totally* want to have sex with me.

4.

There was another book I used to read in Waldenbooks
while standing up, but I finally gave in and bought it.
It was called *The Rape of the A*P*E* (American Puritan
Ethic: The Official History of the Sex Revolution, 1945–
1973: The Obscening of America, an R.S.V.P. Document)*. A
nonfiction cultural survey of American attitudes toward

sex, it was written by Allan Sherman, of "Hello, Muddah, Hello, Fadduh" fame. It was an odd book and my sister rightfully mocked my compulsive reading of it, but one passage remains lodged in my brain.

Every man knows, deep down, that a woman who wants to have sex can find someone to have sex with her. Men have no such confidence. Women can get laid anytime they want to. Men cannot.

This is (a) paraphrased, (b) terribly heteronormative, and (c) almost certainly not true. But my hunch is that it *feels* true to many men, especially men who can't get laid.

I don't know how many men subscribe to this idea, and correlation isn't causation, but the incel coping handbook probably includes these tips:

Make women feel bad about themselves all the time.

Have impossible standards for female beauty.

Seize control of women's bodies however possible and, yes, that includes anti-abortion laws.

Invent high-def television and social media so women will be constantly bombarded with unflattering images of themselves.

A few weeks ago, Christie Brinkley, the unattainable standard of beauty in my twenties, posed in a bathing suit to show how great a sixty-something woman can look in a bathing suit. You should read the comments. Men complained that she was showing off, that she was needy, that she should get over herself. (Obviously, you shouldn't read the comments.)

We literally cannot win with these guys, and by "we" I mean anyone who wants an authentically feminist candidate in 2020. So I'm denying them the privilege to judge me; only I can judge me. *I'm beautiful and I like my body.* Perhaps that is not a popular opinion. I'm okay with that. I have lots of unpopular opinions. I adore chardonnay. I collect visionary art. I am not fond of the novels of Ian McEwan. Anthony Hopkins was the worst Hannibal Lecter.

I have decided I like the way I look and I'm the expert. Who has spent more time looking at me than I have?

5.

I no longer own my copy of *The Rape of the A*P*E**, but another mass market paperback has traveled with me from Evanston, Illinois, to Waco, Texas, to San Antonio, Texas, to Baltimore and remains in my office to this day. In the book's most indelible scene, a woman stands in a neighbor's freezing apartment, compulsively wolfing down cookies. She cannot eat just one cookie because she can never eat just one cookie. She eats all the cookies, rationalizing that her neighbor, who has left his keys in her care while he is away, might not remember he had any cookies if there are no cookies at all.

This is not a novel. It is Susie Orbach's *Fat Is a Feminist Issue*, published in 1978. As Orbach wrote in the *Guardian* on the occasion of the book's fortieth anniversary, she is dismayed that it's still in print, still relevant. Having identified the problem—women use compulsive overeating to soothe themselves in a world where too many demands are placed on them—she hoped the problem would be solved. It wasn't. The fact that her book is still in print is a kind of failure, a rare thing for an author to say.

My plan—eat what I want, when I want—is cribbed from Orbach's advice and the work of eating disorders expert Geneen Roth. It should be simple.

But Orbach, in her *Guardian* essay, zoomed in on an

important development in the processed food industry: The makers of junk food are creating snacks that disrupt our natural sense of satiety. These Frankenfoods are designed to make us want more even when we're full.

So if you like the occasional bag of Utz Cheese Curls— and, boy, do I—you have to accept that it is the food equivalent of being diddled by an incel. To paraphrase a favorite Steve Earle song, you won't ever be satisfied. Recognize that there are billion-dollar industries that cannot be billion-dollar industries if they can't create this dissonance, if they can't persuade people to want what they don't want.

Eat what you want when you want. It sounds simple. But many of the women I know seldom ask themselves what they really want. Women of my generation, in particular, still grapple with all their appetites. As I write this, I am sitting at my dining room table, feeling the day's first flicker of hunger. What do I want? There are doughnuts on the kitchen counter, fancy ones. Do I want those? *No, I'll crash and burn in a few hours.* Do I want another cup of coffee? *I don't know.* What about the leftover frittata from last night's dinner? *I don't know, I don't know, I don't know.*

Eventually I eat a fried egg sandwich. It is exactly what I want.

6.

As it turns out, *The Greengage Summer*, the book that held me in its thrall in a corner of Waldenbooks, begins with compulsive overeating: "On and off, all that hot French August, we made ourselves ill from the green-gages."

"Greengages" are plums. "We" are five English siblings, living in a hotel in Marnes while their mother recuperates from a horsefly bite. The story is told by Cecil, thirteen during the greengage summer. By Chapter 5, the kitchen boy, Paul, has "casually and calmly" put his hands under Cecil's dress, felt her breasts, then said with a dismissive laugh: "Deux petit citrons." Cecil is insulted.

"He laughed again at the outraged look on my face and, with his finger, tapped my nose as one would a little animal if it were too eager."

I think when life gives you *petit* lemons, you should make lemonade—and refuse to share it with people who treat you rudely. I think Cecil should have reached into the kitchen boy's pants, casually and calmly, given his testicles a nice tug, and offered her own fruit comparison. *Deux petit pommes*. Wormy, mealy apples at that.

Ah well, the kitchen boy comes to a bad end. And the novel is really about Cecil's older sister, sixteen-year-old Joss, whose nubile beauty brings out the worst in their reluctant hostess, Mademoiselle Zizi, who sees the girl as a rival. Because, obviously, older women are driven mad by beautiful young women. Everyone knows old women are disgusting. I recently listened to an NPR show—NPR!—with a series of punch lines about granny panties, Angela Lansbury, and what was intended to be a gross-out image of an old woman in a crotchless thong. Every day, everywhere I go, the culture is keen to remind me how repulsive I am.

I thump the culture on the chest, push back, and say one of the most infuriating things a woman can ever say: *Actually, I like the way I look.*

7.

I am gorgeous, but I am not perfect. Since September 24, 2018, 11:42 A.M., I have slipped a few times from the path of my non-journey. I bought a book with a title so stupid I can't bear to tell you its name. And I signed up for Cooking Light's "diet," but only for the healthy recipes. I pick and choose from the weekly eating plans, selecting dinner recipes, ignoring the breakfast and lunch suggestions. I Googled "best swimsuits for women over 50." I bought three. None of them has a skirt and one is a two-piece.

Memorial Day came, the pool opened, and I showed up in one of my new suits, a flattering cut, but not one of those "slimming" brands that make you feel as if you're wearing a whalebone corset. I looked great. Then I noticed—*everyone* looked great.

That's the final step in accepting one's gorgeousness. You then have to concede everyone is gorgeous. You have to turn off that judgey voice in your head, cease making comparisons, stop congratulating yourself on whatever tickets you won in the genetic lottery, while bemoaning the gifts that weren't bestowed. Let your eyes drink everyone in. Don't be like Mademoiselle Zizi in Godden's novel, unnerved by anyone younger, prettier, skinnier. Eat all the greengages you *want*.

8.

Remember the dance teacher who told me I had a pot-belly? In my senior year of high school, I was in the chorus for *Carousel*. The choreographer did not choose me to be part of the dance troupe, which was fair, because I sucked. Weeks passed and she never got around to making up any dance steps. The director sacked her and hired my old dance teacher to whip the show into shape. She immediately asked me to join the dance troupe.

"But I'm not that good," I said.

"No, you're not," she agreed. "But you work hard and you do whatever I tell you to do. I'll get what I need out of you."

I still remember the boy who was tasked with the job of lifting me during "June is Bustin' Out all Over." David Boyd—I'm pretty sure that was his name, his face is more vivid to me—was a quiet blond, lithe and athletic, and every girl in Wilde Lake High School should have been in love with him. One long Sunday, the dance teacher made me run at him again and again and again until, finally, we found the equilibrium that made it possible for him to lift me.

Our dance teacher shouted: "YOU CAN THANK ME FOR THOSE BICEPS, DAVID BOYD." Surely I was the one to be thanked?

A lift requires both dancers to do their parts correctly. In the end, it won't matter how light the female partner is if she can't muster the confidence to run, hit her mark, and leap. (You've seen *Dirty Dancing*, I presume.) I was five-foot-nine and solid as a linebacker. And, it should be noted, beautiful. Prom photos, graduation night photos all show a lovely young woman.

That's the cliché, right? Nora Ephron advised young women to put on bikinis and keep them on until they turn thirty-four, a rather arbitrary cut-off, but it's Ephron, I suppose the arbitrariness is part of the "joke." All the women I know look at old photos and say, "Da-yum," or words to that effect. We are Mademoiselle Zizi *and* Joss both, forever competing with our younger selves.

But if you believe you looked good when you were younger, then simply imagine your future self in a parallel universe, studying 2019 photos and saying, "Da-yum," at how you look now. Stop waiting. Stop entrusting praise to others, especially to sad deluded men who think our bodies are theirs to judge. It is not the trolls or the blunt dance teachers or even our partners who get to tell us we are beautiful. No one can lift us up until we choose to leap.

Back up. Take a running start, launch yourself not at another person, but at a soft bed or sofa or even a swimming pool. Consider, as you leave terra firma, saying those dangerous, forbidden words out loud. Pick any of the sentences I have peppered throughout this piece, knowing how subversive they are for someone who is sixty: *I am a knockout. They totally want to have sex with me. I'm gorgeous. I look great.* Do you know how hard those words were to type, how often I flinched? But I wrote them, I say them without a flicker of irony, and, go figure, I'm finally beginning to believe them.

Game of Crones

1.

My daughter was ten days old the first time I was asked if I was her grandmother.

It was the second week of an unseasonably early Baltimore heat wave and I had managed to maneuver her stroller across my neighborhood's bumpy, narrow sidewalks to my favorite coffee shop. Almost nine years later, I still remember the one spot on our street where the juxtaposition of a tree planter and a set of rowhouse steps made it physically impossible to push a stroller through at any angle. One either had to lift the stroller a foot in the air or bump it over the curb into the street, a solution I figured out only after much grunting and maneuvering. By the time I arrived at the coffee shop, I was sweaty and unkempt.

A young man peered into the stroller, then glanced at my face: "Oh, are you her grandmother?" Only three days earlier, a woman had seen me boarding a plane with my newborn, eyed me approvingly, and whispered: "You look amazing!" An unearned compliment—my daughter didn't come out of my body—but I had been happy to take it. I'm not dumb. I knew the grandmother question would be asked again and again, and that compliments would be rare.

I tried out a simple, direct reply, the one I use to this day: "No, I'm her mother, but I am old enough to be her grandmother, so it's understandable that you would ask."

I thought my answer generous. But in the years since my daughter was born, I have discovered that people who ask rude questions feel terribly affronted if you say anything that implies they have just asked a rude question.

"But I've seen that baby with a young couple," the man said. "Out and about in the neighborhood."

"I don't think so."

"No, I absolutely have," he insisted. "She's been going around with a young couple."

I let it go. I live in a city that, year in and year out, has a startlingly high teenage pregnancy rate, and consequently a high number of young grandmothers, some of whom end up raising their grandchildren. I'd be proud to be one of those women. But I am not. I'm just an old mom and I'm cool with that. Say a word or a phrase often enough, and it loses its power. I'm an old mom. I'm sixty. I'm a sixty-year-old woman with a third-grader. I am old. I am sixty. I am old. I am old. I am old.

"You don't look old to me," my daughter has said on more than one occasion. "You could be in your forties, your thirties, you could be in college, you could be in high school."

Uber drivers say something similar, but at least I know why they're blowing smoke up my ass. I'm not sure what my daughter wants, but she's been eyeing the American Girl doll spaceship, which lists at $449.99 on eBay. Good luck with that, honey. Mama's got money, but she's not *crazy*.

2.

The case against late motherhood is obvious: the later you become a mother, the more likely you are to die while your child is young. Energy levels drop, or so they tell me; the Minnesota Multiphasic Personality Inventory, which I was forced to take by my former employer, labeled me abnormally energetic. But old age also brings a dip in oxytocin, the "nurturing" hormone. There must be a reason that nature cuts women off from reproducing, even as it allows men to keep going.

But nature has reasons for lots of things that we cheerfully circumvent. (The global market for erectile dysfunction drugs is forecast to top $7 billion by 2024.) And while it wasn't exactly my idea to become a mom at fifty-one—more on that in a moment—I think old motherhood has advantages if you're (a) relatively healthy and (b) relatively wealthy. I am lucky enough to be both of those things. Even without my husband's income, I could afford to raise a kid, although, like most Americans, I would be wiped out by a serious illness and college tuition would require most of my retirement fund. I was brought up by Southerners who believe it's tacky to talk about money, but to not talk about money in this situation is disingenuous. To become a mother at age fifty-one is the entitlement cherry on the privilege sundae. It's *greedy*.

I'm not greedy. I didn't want to have it all. To me, life was like a Skee-Ball game at a boardwalk arcade: You banked your shots, collected your tickets, and redeemed them for the best prizes in your point range. I wanted a career (novelist) and a rowhouse (I'm a Baltimorean). And, assuming I had any tickets left over, an interesting, stimulating life partner. By 2002, I had all of those things.

Less than a decade later, motherhood came for me.

3.

I chose the passive voice above, but motherhood at age fifty-one is anything but passive. If you become a mom after the age of fifty, chances are you worked pretty hard. You and a whole army of people—an adoption agency, lawyers, a fertility clinic. Whatever path you choose, the baby is a commodity, something you buy. That sounds cold, but I appreciated the transparency—the delineated costs, the fees paid up front. If you want to have a kid, you might as well get used to opening your wallet. I'm going to keep hammering at this topic, I'm afraid. Money made motherhood possible for me.

Here's how motherhood happened to me. I was in my forties, living with a man who had a delightful son, one of the best people I know. But my partner, now my husband, wanted another child. I mention this because the people who don't assume I'm a grandmother often assume I wanted my "own" baby. They said as much to my face, so lord knows what they said behind my back.

But the man who would become my second husband desired a child, so I made a child happen. That's our dynamic. He writes checks; I make things happen. As noted, I have money of my own, but he out-earns me by a factor of ten-to-one, so this arrangement seems fair to me.

It took me a while, though, to make a baby happen. It took six years, which I found daunting. With each passing year, the refrain in my head changed: I was going to be fifty-nine at the bat mitzvah, then sixty at the bat mitzvah, then sixty-one at the bat mitzvah . . .

Now, God willing and with the help of a good Hebrew tutor, the bat mitzvah will be in four years, when I'm sixty-four, and I find it hilarious that I ever cared. Will she still need me, will she still feed me? She insists the former will apply. She wants me to go to college with her. That idea has merit, although I assume it will be off the table when she's actually eighteen.

Besides, I want to continue writing novels as long as I can. My father retired at sixty-six and it didn't suit him. He died at age eighty-five, but he hadn't been his real self for at least five years. My mother, now eighty-eight and terrifyingly healthy, says women are better suited to retirement. I don't plan to find out, but then my entire life has been spent testing the old maxim, *Man plans, God laughs.*

I have to think God, in whom I don't really believe, busted a gut when my daughter arrived. Lord knows, quite a few other people were laughing at me, filled with barely disguised glee at the belief that I had destroyed my career.

4.

It was Mother's Day, 2010, and I was going to be a mom in less than three weeks, although I didn't know that at the time. Oh, I knew it was imminent—after all, I had orchestrated everything. I had almost finished preparing my daughter's room, making essential purchases. At a family gathering, I ventured an opinion about something I hoped to do as a parent, and a sort-of relative grinned maliciously. "Oh, we can't wait to hear all *your* views on motherhood," she said.

The woman who said this to me was one of the people who had accused me of wanting my "own" baby, who had, unsolicited, urged me not to become an older mother. (She considered herself one and had regrets.) Over lunch several months earlier, she had said: "I can tell you this much about having a kid: You won't write a book a year anymore."

At that moment, I became determined to keep writing a book a year, no matter what.

Spoiler alert: I didn't.

Before I agreed to add a baby to our household, I had conducted a small inquiry in my field, crime fiction. It's a profession that skews old, or did then. And, at the time, there were almost no working mothers among the writers I knew. I approached friends, women, who didn't have children, but no one I asked had ruled kids out because they were career-enders. However, the small coterie of crime writers with young children did end up slowing down their output *if they were women.* A brilliant young writer I knew had stopped publishing when her daughter was three. "It was worth it," she told me via email.

I wasn't so sure. But then—I was almost a decade into my career and I was, am, crazy ambitious. I was thirty-eight when my first book was published, an age some would have considered late for motherhood, and way too late for any literary wunderkind cred. By the time I agreed to have a child, I had published ten books. In 2007, a year out from the year we expected to become parents—we hit a snag and had to start over—I published my first *New York Times* bestseller. There was no way I was getting off that merry-go-round.

As we have seen, there's a lot of math in older motherhood. Here's some more: I used to be able to write a ninety-thousand-word novel in eleven months. Since my daughter was born, I have written some novels at that pace, but I also have allowed myself up to sixteen months to complete others. In her first eight years on the planet, I wrote seven novels, and I should finish another one before she turns ten, knock wood. (I also wrote a children's book, but it literally took forty minutes.) So, no, I no longer write a book a year, but it's fucking close. Besides, it's not my kid who's slowing me down, it's my own ambition, my determination to try to write a different, better book every time.

And, yes, this schedule requires money and help: a full-time babysitter for the first four years of my daughter's life, then Montessori school and a part-time babysitter, now an aftercare program and an assistant who is my childcare fallback. I also depend on the give-and-take of other moms in my neighborhood, who come to each other's aid all the time. On a February snow day, a friend asked if I wanted her to take my daughter to a drop-in art camp. I had already made arrangements, but the mere fact that another person was thinking of me made me want to break down in happy tears.

This was a tough winter, with constant interruptions to my writing schedule, almost all of them child-centric. School closings, school delays, school holidays, illness. And, every regular day, there's the sheer mental space given over to one's child—meals, laundry, moods, homework. (You may wonder where my husband is during all of this. My husband's work as a television producer means he is out of town Monday through Friday, February to mid-September. I hope you enjoy your premium cable content.)

But, somehow, my work gets done. I think that, too, is a function of being older, of knowing that I've done this twenty-three times before, so why shouldn't I be able to do it again? I wrote when I had a full-time job, I wrote when I was going through a divorce, I wrote when I was enduring such a terrible time at my day job that I ground my teeth until my back molars cracked and I spat them into my hand. I wrote when my dog died. I wrote on vacations. I wrote when my household was bouncing back and forth between two cities because of my husband's job. I was back at my writing desk five days after my father died.

In 1999, I was on a panel with Mary Higgins Clark, the writer who basically invented domestic suspense, the subgenre that encompasses all the Girl/Woman/Wife/Sister/Daughter books of today. I was a reporter at the *Baltimore Sun* and I was writing books by getting up at six and putting in two hours before heading to my job. I credited my then-husband for his support, although he was far from the househusband I claimed he was. That

was the public face I put on our incomprehensible relationship. In fact, our marriage was already pretty shaky.

A woman in the audience, her voice heavy with sar-
casm, commented: "Well, that's very nice for you, but
what do we do if we don't have househusbands, if we
have jobs and children?"

Clark, who had started writing as a young widow with
five children, pounded the table cheerfully and said:
"You get the work done when you can do it. You write at
night, you get up at four A.M., but *you get the job done*."

Clark died this year. In case it's not clear, I fucking
worshipped her.

5.

The year my daughter was born, I started buying robots fashioned from cast-off kitchen objects. I now have
what I call my robot army, an assembly of soldiers made
from old coffee cans and thermoses and flatware, many
of them arrayed on a windowsill in my office. I identify
with robots. When I was a child, my mother told me I
was a Venusian robot who would be summoned back to
my home planet when I turned thirteen. That made more

sense to me than anything I heard in the Presbyterian church growing up. A good friend, who didn't even know this story, teases me about my desire to be good, do right, make no mistakes. "You're such a good little robot."

Yet motherhood has made me less robotic, more inclined toward improvisation and spontaneity. We are told that people become rigid with age, fixed in their routines. Even in my thirties, I was so famously monotonous that I compared myself to a hamster. "I would be very happy," I told my newspaper colleagues, "going around and around in my little wheel." My husband gave me a battery-powered one that sits on my desk.

But when one has a young child, routine is a necessity and yet also a luxury. Life, God, whatever you want to call it, kicks my calendar in the shins on a regular basis. My favorite recent "emergency" was Valentine's Day. Yes, I knew it was coming. I didn't understand my daughter was expected to bring twenty-four cards to class until I saw a post on the school's Facebook page late on February 12. That took three hours out of my workday on February 13.

Still, somehow, the work gets done. And not just the work. I'm reading more for pleasure because my daughter and I read side by side at bedtime. I have taken up newish interests—tennis and Italian. I cook more, delighting in my newfound ability to improvise with whatever food is on hand. Old motherhood is clearly good for me.

I have no idea if it's good for anyone else, including my daughter. Motherhood is a story where I don't control the ending.

Earlier this year, I impulsively picked up three Nerf-like dart guns at the local crafts store. My family spent part of the afternoon chasing each other in circles, stockpiling ammunition, launching sneak attacks. THIS IS THE MOST FUN I'VE EVER HAD, my daughter said. I worry this is true, that there's not enough aimless silliness in our lives. At the age of eight, she has been to Italy, France, Spain, Ireland, the UK, Australia, and New Zealand. Last summer, because of my job, she was on a week-long cruise to Alaska. This summer, because of my job, she will return to Tuscany, her fourth visit. She has stayed in luxury hotels, flown in business class, eaten at five-star restaurants, sat in premium seats at Broadway musicals.

But she says the most fun she ever had was the result of three off-brand dart guns that retailed for $9.99 each. I believe her.

6.

On top of everything else this winter, the winter in which my writing schedule had been the universe's favorite punching bag—one more "snow day" and Baltimore city schools would have started chipping away at spring break—I had an ongoing battle with the Department of Public Works, which neglected to pick up my trash three weeks running.

The first time, I yelled at my city councilman and he sent a lovely man from DPW, who seemed so nervous that I couldn't bear doing that again. Shit rolls downhill and no one is more aware of this than the moms who stand sentry at the bottom of their households' hills.

The third time, I stood on my steps in my bathrobe and screamed at the collectors to take my garbage. They insisted that only the block to the south of me was on their route, but I was relentless and they capitulated. I have now figured out that the sidewalk in front of my house falls into a dead zone outside two routes, so I drag my can to the corner.

But the story I want to tell is the one about the second

time, when I threw my trash in the back of the car and started to drive to one of the city's sanitation lots.

En route, I saw a crossing guard arrive at her post and remembered—*Oh yeah, early dismissal today.* Not a problem for me because I pay $200 a month for a school-based aftercare program. But I had forgotten to pack an extra snack. Again, not a problem. I could grab something from the convenience store opposite the school, drop it off, continue on my way.

Then I thought—heck, I got my pages done today. Why not pick up my kid and take her to a matinee? We made it just in time for the 12:50 showing of *The Kid Who Would be King*; I was disappointed that I didn't qualify for the senior fare, but it turns out that everyone pays $8 on Wednesdays. Although my daughter had gobbled a fast cafeteria lunch at school, I treated her to a personal pizza and a box of Sour Patch Kids, most of which ended up on the bottom of my purse, shedding sugar. We were the only two people in the theater, which gave us license to show our noisy appreciation for this updated version of the Arthurian legend. We laughed, we yelled, we high-fived.

At one point, the modern-day Arthur, Alex in this

version, sits on a hillside, trying to absorb shattering news about his father, a less heroic figure than the boy had been led to believe. The abyss opened for me, as it does for us all from time to time. *I'm going to die. I'm going to cease to exist and while I want to be wrong about this, I don't think there is an afterlife. My afterlife will be in others' memories, mainly my daughter's, if I'm lucky. Who will I be in that story?*

Again: No matter how many novels I write, I won't get to write the end of this one.

Our favorite suburban multiplex has a small arcade with two crane machines, one impossible, one a sure bet. I gave my daughter many quarters—I had just stared into the abyss, after all—and she scored two rubber ducks from the easy machine with one grab. A triumphant day, but I still needed to get rid of the trash.

We headed to the sanitation yard, my original destination. It was cold; a light drizzle was starting. A young man, huddled next to a space heater in the makeshift office, showed me where to put my garbage and asked if I needed help.

No, I said, staring up at the receptacle, which had to be at least eight or nine feet high. *No, I do not.*

And, mindful of my daughter's eyes on me, I hoisted my bag of garbage—a week's worth of trash—and swung it high and hard, giving it all the oomph that my sixty-year-old biceps can pack. Which is, by the way, quite a bit. (I belong to a gym, I work out with a trainer, I've been taking tennis lessons—again, all reminders that health and wealth are amazing privileges.)

"What did that man say to you?" she asked when I got back in the car.

"He asked if I needed help."

"Did you?"

"Nope."

"Did you want help?"

"Nope."

"What did he think?"

"I always tell you, it's a waste of time to try to guess what people are thinking."

"What do you *think* he was thinking?"

"I think he was glad that he didn't have to leave the warmth of his office. And that maybe I needed help because I'm old. But I didn't."

I hope this day lives in her memory—the impromptu movie, the rubber ducks, the rubbery movie theater pizza. But most of all, I hope she remembers her defiantly old mother with that garbage bag. I hope the memory expands and exaggerates, so that in her mind's eye, I whipped that trash around and around in a circle over my head, shouting like a warrior before I let it fly. I hope it's a story she tells her daughter one day, and I don't care how old she is when that happens. Because in asserting for the unexpected pleasures of older motherhood, I am not arguing against motherhood at any other age. I'm not suggesting anyone else live my life. I'm not saying I don't sometimes seethe with resentment over the fact that I am a de facto single mother, but that situation has nothing to do with my age. I won't deny that I have put my head in my hands and wept over another day of work lost. I'm not saying you should have children and I'm not saying you shouldn't. Do what you wanna, as the song goes.

I have said throughout and will continue to say: Money helps. But maybe it's not the big money. Maybe it's the quarters that go into the crane machine, the $8 matinee ticket, the $9.99 off-brand dart gun, the coins stacked on my dining room table as my daughter tries to figure out how much money she needs to buy a knock-off American Girl school room with seventy-six pieces.

(At only $139.99, it's a relative bargain compared to the spaceship, but I'm still not paying for it.) Maybe it's also the money I *don't* earn, the things I don't write because I decide to play hooky for an afternoon. Heck, writing this piece was a loss leader; my per-word rate for fiction is much higher than my rate for nonfiction.

And maybe the next time—there's always a next time, trust me—someone says, "Are you her grandmother?" I'll say: "No I'm her *great*-grandmother, I'm eighty-fucking-seven, but I look amazing for my age."

I am old. I am sixty. I am a sixty-year-old woman with a third-grader. I am old. I am old. I am old. I am sixty, my daughter is eight, and I will let her write the end of the story. What other choice do I have?

Natural Selection

1.

This is how I remember it, as every dubious story begins.

Baltimore likes to boast that it integrated ahead of *Brown v. Board of Education*, the 1954 Supreme Court case argued by native son Thurgood Marshall Jr. True: An African American student was admitted to Polytechnic, one of the city's most prestigious public high schools in 1952.

After the *Brown* ruling, the school district implemented an "open enrollment" policy. Students could attend any school in the city, but if it wasn't the school in the immediate catchment area, transportation was their responsibility. And, while students were free to choose their schools, they weren't always welcome at the schools they chose. The photos of white students protesting at Southern High School are a stark reminder of what a racially divided city Baltimore was, is. Meanwhile, hyper-segregation, a problem in Baltimore to this day, helped preserve majority white schools even as Baltimore became a majority African American school district. By the early 1970s, it was clear that the city would have to develop a less passive form of integration. Rumors abounded.

Four public Baltimore high schools were segregated by gender as well—City College and the aforementioned Polytechnic were boys-only, Western and Eastern for girls. Those schools featured a magnet-like program, the A-course, open to the city's best students. If you qualified for the A-course, you entered high school in the ninth grade, instead of the tenth as was customary until the 1980s. As of 1973, the year I started Western High School, no girl had attended Poly or City, no boy had been admitted to Eastern or Western.

Many of Western's A-course students had been my classmates in elementary school and/or junior high.

Maggie, Lynette, Juanita, Tawna, Robyn, Susan W., Susan C., Cherby, Kasey, Leigh, Erin—we were pretty evenly divided between black and white. (If you had to choose, from the names above, who belonged to which race, you'd almost certainly get it wrong. But why would you want to choose?) We were smart kids, part of our junior high school's "enriched" track, confident and cocky.

At Western, we found ourselves alongside a substantial number of girls from the city's parochial schools. The gossip was that the nuns had conspired to help substandard students get into the A-course so that they would not be caught up in busing, should it come to Baltimore. From a distance of forty-plus years, it is hard to make sense of this rumor, but I think the idea was that once they were in Western, they could drop out of the A-course in tenth grade and avoid being bused to a different, possibly "undesirable" school.

Then another rumor made the rounds, only this one was definitely true. Poly, which shared a courtyard, auditorium, and athletic facilities with Western, would admit its first girl in the fall of 1974, only twenty-two years after its first black student enrolled. Some of my classmates participated in a walk-out—to *protest* coeducation. If a girl attended Poly, it was only a matter of time before a boy enrolled at Western. Boys would inhibit us, they argued. Boys would distract. Better to flirt with them in the courtyard, during our lunch hour, and leave them behind when it was time for academics. I thought my friends ridiculous. We'd have to compete with boys soon enough. Why wait?

Meanwhile, the Catholic girls and a cohort of Protestants with fundamentalist leanings were upset that our ninth-grade social studies class was focused on evolution and natural selection. "I am not descended from apes," one girl told our teacher over and over, although he had said no such thing. "God made me! God made me!"

I wasn't horrified by the prospect of male classmates or the teaching of evolution, but I was confused. I had arrived at high school believing that animals evolved within their life spans, that if a trait was required, the body manifested it. I blame Rudyard Kipling's *Just So Stories*, not the city school system, for my ignorance. How the camel got its hump, how the leopard got its spots, how the elephant got its trunk—the stories were fanciful, but in line with the theories of the early nineteenth century

French naturalist Jean-Baptiste Lamarck. According to Lamarck, if a giraffe needed a long neck to reach foliage, it grew one. Charles Darwin, coming along almost six decades after Lamarck, argued natural selection: long-necked giraffes survived because a long neck favored survival, while short-necked giraffes were weeded from the gene pool. It was silly to think otherwise, our teacher told us. We can't grow something just because we need it.

But why wouldn't adolescent girls believe that animals' bodies changed within a single life span to adapt as survival dictated? At that very moment, our bodies were changing at nature's behest. Our breasts and vulvas were growing, our body fat was redistributing, hair was sprouting in new places. Sex education was mandatory in the sixth grade, at least in public schools, so my friends and I were very clear on what was happening where in our bodies. I'm less sure what the Catholic girls knew.

I am confident that none of us had any understanding that forty years later, give or take, it would happen all over again—changes in breasts, vulvas, and hormones, the redistribution of body fat, hair in new places. And nobody seems to know why. No, seriously, no one. Try Googling "What is the evolutionary point of meno-

pause" and most of the results will default to telling you
what menopause is.

But you will find this abstract of a paper published in
1994:

> With the possible exception of pilot whales, no
> mammals studied to date are known to commonly
> exhibit reproductive cessation in nature.

"With the possible exception of pilot whales"—if you
won't do it for women, science, then think of the whales.
What is the *point* of menopause? What are its advantages, from an evolutionary perspective?

To boil it down to two words: Menopause, why?

2.

"I was going to give you a pair of tweezers," said a friend,
"because now that you're fifty you're going to have to
pluck your chin hairs every day."

"Not to worry," I said. "I've been plucking my chin for
years."

It was the day after a glorious surprise party, engineered

by my husband. I was still five years out from menopause, not that I knew it. Menopause, except for those plunged into it prematurely for medical reasons, does not announce itself. Menopause is a sneaky motherfucker. You amble forward until one day, twelve months after having no menstrual period, you cross an invisible finish line. It's like being one of the laggards in a marathon, although there is no one there to cheer you.

I had my last period in Paratallada, Spain, in August 2013, at the age of fifty-four. This means I was in menopause at the age of fifty-five, a little late for a woman in North America, where the average age is fifty-one. My body, which had never been completely under my control—whose is?—became particularly unruly in menopause, to borrow an adjective from the writer Roxane Gay. I gained weight. My body odor seemed more pronounced. I had hot flashes and night sweats. My sleep was wildly disordered, my moods even more so.

I read somewhere that menopause was intended to make women happy to die. That seems a bit extreme, but then I had, and continue to have, a relatively mild transition, which means entire days go by without me wanting to kill anyone. The hot flashes are terrible, but only I am aware of them. I have been advised to give up wine and caffeine, and I am . . . taking that under advisement. Friends and Lyft drivers tell me I appear at least a decade younger than I am. A lovely compliment, but do the math: At sixty, I look fifty.

At fifty, I looked forty-something. I sat in a New York bar with a Very Famous Actress and we made a solemn vow never to alter our faces with plastic surgery. She has kept the promise and looks gorgeous. I have kept the promise and I look how I look, which is fine with me. I like my face. I feel great about my neck.

Other than the Very Famous Actress, I have few role models for aging without surgery. I love the *Real Housewives* franchise, but it's hard, watching these women begin to pick, pick, pick at their features. Their faces get smoother and puffier, their eyes become slits. It's just as difficult to read *James and the Giant Peach* to my nine-year-old daughter and see those terrifying aunties, Sponge and Spiker, one stout and one stringy, both vicious. Is there any acceptable way for a woman to age?

Of course there is always Madonna, not even a year older than I am, a ubiquitous presence throughout my adult life. There was a period in my twenties when I thought she might go away; by my thirties I was resigned to her staying power, impressed by it. Madonna is to my generation what Elizabeth Taylor was to my mother's—an impossible standard until she isn't.

In the 1970s, Elizabeth Taylor went through a phase of being overweight, to the point where she was satirized by John Belushi on *Saturday Night Live*, choking on an enormous turkey leg. But the crueler joke, I think, was from an uncredited middle-aged woman: "We always wanted to look like Elizabeth Taylor and god help us now we do." Elizabeth Taylor was in her forties at the time.

Madonna would never let herself gain weight. So she is mocked for her hands, her sinew, the plastic surgery she won't "own," her determination to be seen as a sexual being, dating younger men such as Alex Rodriguez. When she is eighty, I'm sure some wag will say, "We always wanted to look like Madonna and now god help us we do."

Menopause doesn't make women want to die. It makes other people wish we would die, or at least disappear. And if we refuse to disappear, they will ridicule us, try to render us invisible, or maybe just flatten us with an enormous piece of stone fruit rolling down a hill.

Then again, they now make tweezers with ingenious little lights, and who's going to buy those if you get rid of all the old women?

3.

When I was eleven or twelve, a child was assaulted in a Baltimore city school, apparently by a stranger. The response in my school was to bring the fifth- and sixth-grade students together for an assembly to watch two films: *Girls Beware* and *Boys Beware*, 1961 propaganda made by a man named Sid Davis.

The rampant homophobia of *Boys Beware* has been mocked by many. *Girls Beware*, the sequel, has its howlers, too. I recently rewatched it, anticipating a good laugh. It features a babysitter taking a gig from a man she didn't know (murdered), a babysitter refusing to admit a man to the house so he could make a phone call (not murdered), a girl accepting a ride home from two strange boys at a movie (raped). Ah yes, these were the coded warnings about stranger danger I expected, down to the female narrator's praise for the good manners of the second babysitter. When turning a would-be rapist and-or murderer away from one's door, one should still be *polite*. There are no pervy uncles or cousins, no inappropriate teachers or odious bosses. In *Girls Beware*, the call is never coming from inside the house.

But the final story in *Girls Beware* holds up. It starts with an older, good-looking teen who likes to hang out at malt shops and burger stands.

Here [Bob] sought out the company of younger teenagers because he wasn't accepted by the company of his own age group . . . Bob enjoyed nothing more than talking about himself . . . As time went on, he became jealous of her friends and insisted on spending more time alone . . . Bob became more and more demanding . . . Mary complied with his desires.

The film does not use the word "pregnant," although that is clearly Mary's problem. She is "entrusted to juvenile authorities." That seems a bit much, but the film's advice about older men is spot-on: *Too many young girls are flattered by the attention of older boys and do not realize that these boys, who cannot compete in their own age group, are often not well adjusted.*

Adult men began following me in the street when I was fourteen, offering me rides. When I was nineteen, a man masturbated in front of me on a Chicago El train during rush hour. In my twenties, I lived in San Antonio and Mexico, where I was often catcalled in the streets. People told me that I would miss this "attention" when it stopped. I didn't, I don't. This attention went on for more than a quarter of a century. It was approximately a quarter century too much.

I blamed myself. On occasion, other women blamed me as well. At the age of twenty-one, I was walking down the street in Chicago, en route to meet a friend, when a salesman at a clothing store grabbed me by the wrist and pulled me into the store. He was at least five years older, well dressed by the disco standards of the day. I sat in a chair, legs demurely crossed at the ankles, enduring his interrogation because I yearned to know what he saw. Had he picked me because I looked naive, an easy mark? Or was it possible that I was actually *pretty*? After ten minutes or so of conversation, I decided it was the former and hurried away, refusing to make plans with him. When I told my friend what had made me late, she rolled her eyes. "Well, of course he stopped you, dressed like that."

I remember what I was wearing, but I won't tell you.

Trust me, it doesn't matter what I was wearing. Fifteen years later, I was sexually harassed by a colleague while wearing an ankle-length dress of polished blue cotton, an outfit that would have been suitable for one of the teen victims in *Girls Beware*. It was never about what I was wearing. It wasn't even about me. That was the hardest lesson to learn.

It was especially confounding when the men had greater status than clothing store salesman. A great-ish American novelist, a syndicated newspaper columnist, a handsome actor, a lobbyist, a poet, a national correspondent for one of the country's best newspapers.

I wasn't flattered. Well, maybe by the handsome actor, who was content to stare at my ass as if he had never seen one of that size and heft. I was a target, lined up in a scope. To be someone's prey is not flattering. Does the deer thank the hunter for choosing her?

Luckily—it's important to lean into that word, "*luckily*"—the creeps I met took "No" for an answer. Years later, I ran into the great-ish novelist at a party. I had spent an afternoon with him, profiled him, he had written me what can be described only as a mash note, he told mutual acquaintances I was a "handsome" woman, but now he claimed no memory of me. I believe him. Besides, the important thing is, *I* remember *him*. I remember them all.

I recall even more vividly the female journalist who watched the national correspondent circling me, her sour smile, her condescension at my fledgling status on the beat. She disapproved—of *me*. If my pursuer had been able to inveigle his way into my motel room, as he attempted later, she would have assumed I got what I wanted, or at least what I deserved.

A few years ago, I read her obituary and felt a weird relief. I had learned not to care what men thought. I wasn't real to men. But another woman, only a decade my senior, had watched someone target me and her loyalty was to him, a member of her tribe, the traveling press corps.

Does natural selection explain this, too? I've never been able to work out women's jealousy and envy toward one another. Best I can tell, there is plenty of sperm to go around. Way too much, actually. Based on the economic principle of supply and demand, sperm is worthless. Shouldn't we be like lions, kicking the men out after they impregnate us, keeping only one or two around? Why do women age-shame one another, especially about menopause? *Ha-ha, you can't have babies anymore.* I never could, anyway.

If you're going to link your self-worth to your fertility, you're going to peak at about age twenty-five. Meanwhile, a study released by Rutgers researchers in May 2019 found a host of medical problems associated with older fathers and advised men to bank their sperm by age forty-five if they want to have children. My favorite line in the article I read about the report was this: "The study also found that older men struggle with fertility issues even if their partner is under twenty-five."

I'm more interested in what the female partner is struggling with.

4.

When I was in my late thirties, I bought a thirteen-year-old Toyota Corolla from a friend. Come to think of it, the car might have been seventeen years old. At any rate, it cost $350 and had 115,000 miles on the odometer. My mechanic told me the body would give way before the engine. By the time I junked that car, ever so reluctantly,

I could see the pavement flashing through the corroded floorboards.

I think about that car when I slather moisturizer on my body while watching the *Real Housewives*. A younger friend recently asked me about the relative smoothness of my décolletage, a word I have been waiting a lifetime to use in print. "You have to moisturize like it's your *job*," I said.

The term "self-care" has a complex, decades-old history with roots in radical feminism. However, it jumped in popularity after November 2016 and is now often conflated with its say-nothing sister, "wellness." But it is a *radical* feminist idea and we shouldn't let it be co-opted by capitalism, which wants to sell us the tools of self-care while making us feel crappy about the self that requires this care. *What would happen if a woman told the truth about her life?* Muriel Rukeyser asked, then answered: *The world would explode.* What happens when women take care of themselves, if they decide their bodies belong to them? The world implodes.

I go back, again and again, to those ninth-grade lessons in natural selection. The scientific literature on menopause is over my head, but I am clear on this much: No one knows the "why" of it. There are theories and supposition, but no hard facts. Why do women (and pilot whales) hang around so long after their childbearing years end?

I developed my own menopause theory. If a species is hell-bent on reproducing itself, then sperm is wasted on the infertile. But you know men, they'll hump whatever is handy in a pinch. An elderly rancher in my favorite Larry McMurtry novel literally fucks the land. A Texas man on the side of a highway, caught in flagrante with a chicken, claimed he got out of his car to urinate and the chicken emerged from nowhere and plopped itself on his dick. (I read the police report as a young cop reporter, but it was decided the paper could not run such a story.) If older women are going to have the temerity to be attractive, how do we keep men with vital sperm away from them? Good God, think of all that sperm Alex Rodriguez wasted on Madonna. Nature must be beside herself. And don't kid yourself, he's wasting it on Jennifer Lopez, too, now that she's fifty. Nature doesn't care if you look good for your age. Nature is not impressed with your self-care rituals. Nature doesn't give a fuck if the planet is overpopulated. Nature wants that seed to find *purchase*.

So let's offer men some visual and tactile clues on whom to avoid if they want to create babies. Make menopausal women look like men (hair on chin, upper lip). Make them look pregnant (protruding bellies). Make procreational sex unpleasant for them and their partners (dry vaginas). Make the women themselves unpleasant (plummeting levels of oxytocin, hot flashes, mood swings).

"God made me! God made me!" insisted the terrified girl in my ninth-grade social studies class. My other classmates stood up and walked out of school to protest the idea of boy classmates. Forty-five years later, no boy has ever attended Western High School; the Baltimore city school system has declined to explain to me how this is possible. The other all-girl high school, Eastern, is long gone; the all-boy schools, Poly and City, are now majority female. I wanted to compete with boys because I knew I would have to compete with them in the world at large. Yet they didn't see me then and they don't see me now. My classmates were on to something, even as I scoffed. We didn't need to be around boys 24-7. Maybe we didn't need them at all.

My body is changing. I don't know why. Best I can tell, nobody knows why. It turns out we're not even sure why the giraffe has a long neck. One camp insists it was to reach for foliage. Another says it's because the male giraffe uses his neck to attract the female by "clubbing." Yet a third theory suggests that giraffes' long necks help them stay cooler.

A long neck can keep one cooler? Please let my neck grow. I imagine all the menopausal women, our necks stretching, stretching, stretching like Alice in Wonderland, which would give us the extra advantage of being able to see our predators, a theory about the giraffe's neck that has been discredited. But how lovely it would be to gaze down at everyone from a great height, to tower over those who have tried to discount us. Apologies to my ninth-grade teacher, but my personal history tells me that my body adapts, will continue to adapt, and—heresy of heresies, folly of follies—that I will have a say in how it adapts.

The Art of Losing Friends and Alienating People

1.

I am firmly in the camp that believes we need new interests and new goals as we age. At sixty, I have taken up tennis and am dutifully working my way through Duolingo's basic Italian lessons. Recently, a friend and I decided to pursue Stephen Sondheim completist status, attending productions of every musical for which he has written music and/or lyrics. Alas, our crowded calendars keep us from being as nimble as we need to be. *Passion* in the Philippines would have been amazing, but we couldn't even make it to *The Frogs* in suburban Detroit. Clearly, we're going to be at this for a while.

But this past spring, we managed to bag a New York production of *Merrily We Roll Along*, a Sondheim work that has been vexing dramaturges since its original 1981 Broadway run of only sixteen performances. Based on the 1934 play of the same name by George S. Kaufman and Moss Hart, it moves backward in time, centering on a three-way friendship that has fractured beyond repair. Mary, who always had a thing for Frank, has become a bitter alcoholic. Frank has ignored the work he does best, composing, in order to become a mogul, at which he is mediocre. Frank and Charley no longer speak at all. Because the story moves from their crabby old age (forty-something!) to their more hopeful twenties, we see the fallout before we hear the bomb. The suspense is not fueled by whether Frank and Charley will patch things up, but by the origin of the feud. Who did what to whom?

That reveal comes quickly, one advantage of a backward-moving story. The fifth or sixth song, depending on the production you see—people are forever tinkering with *Merrily*—is a bravura rant. Charley breaks down on a live television show while discussing his writing partnership with Frank. *Which comes first*, Charley is asked, *the words or the music?* The contract, he replies, then launches into "Franklin Shepard, Inc.," a laundry list of his friend's shortcomings.

The song builds, his rage builds. But just as Charley appears on the verge of one of those musical theater transitions that was mocked in *Spamalot*'s "The Song That Goes Like This," he stops himself and begins to speak-sing softly. He misses Frank. He wants him back.

His argument is contradictory. He compares friendship to a garden that has to be tended, then, shades of Elizabeth Bishop, says, "Friendship's something you don't really lose." The tempo begins to build. He's out of control and he knows it. *Very sneaky how it happens . . . Oh my god, I think it's happened. Stop me quick before I sink.* He ends with a few vicious, well-chosen words about Frank's obsession with money. The friendship is irrevocably broken. It's unclear what can't be forgiven—the stinging words or the public airing of the grievance.

Absent this kind of betrayal or falling-out, most friendships don't end so definitively. These no-ending endings can be hard to process. Our culture long ago made peace with the fragility of matrimony, but we still have high expectations for friendships. If you really care about someone, you should be able to pick up where you left off, no matter how long it's been. Friendship's something you don't really lose, right?

Hold my beer, Charley. It's Frank's turn to sing.

2.

My Charley did not opt for a flame-out on live television, or even a private delineation of my failings as a friend. My Charley disappeared so quietly that when I finally realized she was gone, I was thrust into an endless hindsight loop. I became a forensic IT analyst, gathering clues from email, social media, and annual holiday cards—or the lack thereof.

In my defense, it's difficult to realize that one has been ghosted when the ghoster disdains all forms of social media. My Charley had long ago made it clear that we would never find her in those vapid precincts, no, no, no. I admired her for this stance because no one admires people *not* on social media more than people like myself, who are on social media just a little bit too much. No FOMO for the holdouts. Their brains, untouched by social media's jangly rhythms and assaults, can focus. I would love to be like, say, my friend Andre Dubus III, who uses a flip phone and is vividly, insistently present in the world. I start the day by checking email; Andre reads a poem.

But—but, but, but, but, but, *but*—despite all the damage they've wrought, despite Cambridge Analytica and Fake News and the indifference to the rape/death threats made against women and people of color, Facebook and Twitter have their merits. They've kept me sane. As the old mother of a young child with a hardworking husband whose job forces him to be away from home pretty regularly, I see social media as my lifeline and party line, a way of plugging into like-minded communities. On Twitter, I talk about books, television, and politics. On Facebook, I tend toward the *Real Housewives* and kale. I'm old enough to remember when socially obtuse people pulled out the Kodak Carousel after a dinner party and made you endure slides of their vacation. Now I volunteer for that experience, sitting at my computer and "hearting" my way through Facebook photos. Babies, graduates, prom-goers, sunsets, gardens. The novel was once mocked as dangerous, lightweight entertainment for women. Maybe social media is getting the same bum rap.

In October 2018, two friends on the other side of the

country lost their teenage daughter to cancer. Because of Facebook, I could follow Evie from diagnosis to treatment, observe my friends career from hope to despair to hope to devastation. When the time came that there was nothing but bad news, I was grateful that they had a forum where they could share the updates efficiently. I was more grateful still that they continued to write about Evie after her death, sharing photos and memories of her. Real life is anxious for the bereft to move on, to heal. Social media, for all its flibberty-gibberty attention span, doesn't put an expiration date on grief.

And, yeah, sure, social media is full of bots and trolls who will, say, dox you and investigate your Jewish origins and call you a pervert for teaching your six-year-old the word "vagina." Social media is a hellscape. Social media is a place where people fake being successful when they are falling-apart messes. Social media, best I can tell, is exactly like life.

As noted, my Charley isn't on social media, but her husband is. Back when I thought Charley and I were still friends, I would check his page to glean what was going on with her. Then, about four years ago, I stumbled on the fact that the husband and I were no longer Facebook friends.

At first I assumed it was a technical glitch; perhaps he had started a new account and was rebuilding his contacts. *Do you know [x]? To see what he shares with friends, send him a friend request.* But, no, all our mutual friends were still linked to him. I alone had been jettisoned.

Only—when? Why? I racked my brain for an offense. I searched my email for my last communication with her. (Cordial, a quick reply to her request for information, but also a passing reference to an actual letter I had written for her birthday.) My conscience was, is, clear-ish.

There are mutual friends who might have information, but it seems unfair to involve them. To discuss the rift would be to create sides. There are no sides here. She's done with me and that's a legitimate choice. I made one indirect appeal, an openhearted gesture intended to demonstrate how much I respected and valued her. It went unacknowledged.

But I'm a mystery writer and this mystery tugs at me: Why do friendships end? Why did this friendship end? How do any friendships survive a life span? Do any friendships last a lifetime? Do I have any real friends? How bad a friend am I?

Pretty bad, actually. We'll get to that.

3.

"Do you know," I asked my trainer, "that there's a theory about how many friends one can really have? It was developed by an anthropologist, Robin Dunbar, who did a TED talk on the topic."

"Five close ones, right?"

"I think that's right. And then you can have a community of up to a hundred and fifty. How many do you have? Close friends?"

"Three."

"Does that include your wife?"

"No, I put her in a different category."

"Same," I said of my husband. "Close friends, I think I have four. There are basically four people who know everything about me. Then six to ten others who know a lot."

"But how many would help you bury a body?"

"Oh, then it's only three. Nancy simply could not help me commit a crime."

We fell silent as I did mountain climbers. My trainer, Todd, has been part of my life for almost fifteen years. I am his mother's age. When we first started working together, he was a twenty-something bro; now he's married, with two young children. He knows everything about me. *Everything.* He was at my surprise fiftieth birthday party. I was at his wedding. Our relationship is contained within twice-weekly hour-long sessions; it is rare for us to see or speak to each other outside that window, although we text about the schedule, share recipes, and, yes, follow each other on social media.

He is kind, capable, and unflappable. He hunts deer with a bow and arrow, feasting on the venison throughout the winter. He has a garden and goats and chickens and a generator and if the shit ever goes down, when the zombie apocalypse is upon us, I am driving straight to Todd's house with my husband and child.

I think he might be one of my best friends.

He would definitely help me bury a body. Although he would probably make me do most of the digging because it would be a good upper-body workout.

4.

As a friend, I frequently break the first rule of fiction: I'm all tell, no show. I'm not going to remember your kid's birthday, or even yours, despite Facebook's helpful nudges. When you're in a crisis, I won't know the right questions to ask. I blame my Southern parents for placing so many topics in the forbidden zone. I grew up being told it was rude to discuss age, income, health, feelings. I often think that's why I became a reporter.

I have a list in my head of all the friends I let down. It's not long, but it's longer than I'd like, and it's probably longer than I know. Most of those friends have forgiven me, but I never lose sight of my failures. It's like a stain on a busily patterned rug; once you know where to look, your eye goes there every time. I know where to look. I am aware of my misdeeds. Every friend who has ever called me out on being a bad friend had me dead to rights.

But this does not apply to Charley, who enumerated my flaws only when I demanded that she do so. More than a decade ago, she retreated, seemingly done with me. I pursued, asking what I had done wrong. She ticked off my sins: self-centered, shallow, superficial, materialistic. I was taken aback and a little defensive, but I could see her side of things, so I apologized. And it wasn't a mealymouthed *if-you-feel-offended-then-I'm-sorry* apology. It was full-throated and sincere, a *mea* culpa that was all *mea*. Later, I found out she had gone through a huge crisis at about the time of our break and I thought that explained everything.

I went through an awful time during the eighteen-month period in which I managed to get ghosted without noticing. Most of my friends know little about it. (My trainer has all the details.) My friend of longest duration—Nancy, who really would have a hard time helping me bury a body—was told almost nothing. Inevitably, she's one of the friends I let down, too, more than twenty years ago, but she forgave me. The longer you know me, the greater the odds of me failing you. Nancy has come to understand that my worst predilection as a friend is—oh, irony of ironies—disappearing with no explanation when I'm unhappy.

We've known each other for forty-five years, Nancy and I, yet I still want to protect her from my worst self, my self-pitying self. I'm not sure why. In part it's because I am mathematically eliminated from what she has, a marriage that will soon enter its fifth decade. I was her bridesmaid, barely a month after we graduated college. I thought she was insane. But she has one of Those Marriages, the kind that makes everyone feel vaguely inadequate. My first marriage lasted seven years. I have been with my second husband for nineteen years, under the same roof for seventeen, married for thirteen. To make it to five wedded decades together, we have to live into our late nineties. Nancy could be on her eighth decade of marriage by then.

"You know I'm always there for you," Nancy said the last time we managed to get together after a long hiatus. "I want to hear from you when things aren't going well." I do know. But, without the lubrication of alcohol or sweat, without the buffer of a computer screen and a DM box, I find it hard to share my troubles. Maybe that results in my life looking shinier, easier than it is. I don't know. I am achingly aware of my luck—the career of my dreams, no real money worries (although I think every sentient American should worry about being bankrupted by health issues), having a family late in life. The things that go wrong for me are so clearly my fault. I don't deserve anyone's sympathy, ever.

But the worst thing about me is that, as a friend, I'm a terrible novelist. I can't stop creating narratives about my friends. These stories are almost always positive and uplifting. What's wrong with that? you might ask. Well, it means I'm closing the book on my friends, seeing their lives, their journeys, as finished. Did I do that to the friend who ghosted me? Yes, I did. I tidied up all the messy strands in her life and put her on the shelf, another mystery solved.

To be clear, this is absolutely a shitty thing to do.

"So what's my narrative?" asked my oldest friend, Nancy.

"That you were the sane one in your crazy family, that you were so lacking in role models that you had to figure out everything for yourself."

She conceded this was basically true, but also told me that I must stop writing "happily ever after" at the end of my friends' stories. People's stories are never finished, not as long as they're alive.

They don't even end with death.

5.

On June 28, 2018, an armed gunman walked into the newsroom of the Annapolis *Capital Gazette* and killed five people. I was on the road, driving to my mother's house—I had been on the highway that passes through Annapolis about the time of the shooting. When I heard the news, I knew there was a good chance my friend Rob Hiaasen was one of the victims.

For the next ninety minutes, I drove as phone calls poured through my dashboard bluetooth connection from all over the country. I had met Rob when we worked at the *Baltimore Sun,* and our former colleagues, all reporters, were doing the only thing they could do in a crisis, report. From a Michigan vacation, one friend looked at Rob's social media pages. He had not checked in safe, so we decided that Rob wasn't much for social media. In New York, my husband was using his access to staffers at the *New York Times* to try to get the casualty list; Rob was one of the unconfirmed victims. Still, it was unconfirmed. The *Times* wasn't ready to print it.

My car's tires were crunching on the seashells of my mother's driveway when the final call came. Rob was officially dead. I burst into tears and said to the friend who had called with the news: "I knew it. He was just so fucking tall."

Rob was, I think, six-foot-six. For six years, 1994–2000, we had sat within three feet of each other in the *Baltimore Sun* features section. When I left the newspaper and was presented with the traditional fake page one, he contributed a sardonic piece about the awards I had won as a crime novelist. He used the byline "Rob 'Absolutely No Fucking Relation to Carl' Hiaasen." (The bestselling crime writer was his brother.) Once, for reasons he couldn't explain, Rob took my hand and leaned forward as if to kiss it—and bit me on the knuckle. I thought this was hilarious. I was nine days older than he was and bemused by how much milestone ages weighed on him. He was seven months out from his sixtieth birthday when he died and was probably already dreading it.

I say "probably" because when Rob was killed, I don't think I had seen or spoken to him for almost two years. He was commuting daily to his job, which meant being behind the wheel of his car almost three hours a day. I had a small child. But, no, the burden was on me. I had the easier life, the more flexible schedule. It was my responsibility to reach out to my old friend and say, *Stop by for a beer on your way home one night.* To organize a lunch or dinner. Social media can take a friendship only so far.

In the wake of Rob's death, I was asked to write about him for various publications. I didn't feel good about this. It seemed dishonest, fake. I imagined my other ghost-friend, the still-living one, judging me from afar. *Still all about you, isn't it, Laura? It's so much easier to eulogize a friend than to be one.*

I had finished a novel the day before Rob was murdered. I dedicated it to him and his four colleagues. A year later, the book enjoyed some success and I was interviewed a lot. I was asked about Rob. I didn't expect this, disingenuous as this might sound. Again, I thought about my living ghost and her inevitable disapproval. She had always seemed annoyed with me when I was featured in the press. "Well, that was weird," she had emailed about one profile. That was the entirety of her feedback.

Still all about you, isn't it, Laura?

A year after Rob's death, his friends threw a book party for a collection of his columns that was published posthumously. I had attended a rocky memorial the previous year, one with solipsistic digressions and the airing of dirty laundry. Determined to avoid such well-intentioned sloppiness, I became a bossy bitch, informing the other organizers that we would limit the number of speakers and readers. I didn't feel I deserved to be among the readers, which included Rob's best friend, Kevin, and his wife, Maria, but I took one of the slots when asked.

Afterward, I met a young man who had worked for Rob in Annapolis, before moving on to the *Baltimore Sun*. "Rob talked about you all the time," he said. "Do you remember that podcast interview you did for *The Sun*?" I did, vaguely. "You called him your journalistic soul mate. I told him about it. He was so pleased."

That cheered me slightly, knowing I had articulated my regard for Rob and word had gotten back to him. Still, I can't stop thinking about all the lost opportunities for his company when he was alive. I go back through his Facebook page to the days and weeks before June 28, 2018, looking for moments I should have engaged. I want to affix a heart to everything I see, no matter how mundane. So many smiling photos, so many celebrations of the things he loved—his wife, his children, golf, dogs, a particular Irish pub.

Rob is the ghost I deserve, but he's too generous to haunt me. Then again, maybe we choose our ghosts.

6.

So here I am, belting my own scorched-earth show tune. Careful as I've been to obscure my ghost-friend's identity, she will recognize herself here, should she ever read this. Which seems unlikely, but it turns out she has used her husband's Facebook account as a peephole on the world in which she prefers not to participate. A mutual friend inadvertently let this information slip. I let it go. I am trying to let it go. I still check her husband's page from time to time. *Do you know [x]? To see what he shares with friends, send him a friend request.* Last year, I finally stopped sending them an annual holiday card.

My oldest friend, Nancy, who won't help me bury a body but would get me a good lawyer, said to me during my most recent visit: "Don't you get tired of people saying, '*This is what happens at your age. People die. And you just have to get used to it*'? But I don't want to get used to it."

Boy, do I get tired of it. I am tired of hearing those words. I am tired of having reunions at funerals. I am tired of feeling guilty because it's hard to do right by all the good people I know. There are so many people I love

that I haven't even spoken to in the past year, unless social media exchanges count as speaking. Isn't that part of
getting old, too? Amassing so many friends that you can't
keep up with them? I have my summer camp friends, my
college friends, my Waco friends, my San Antonio friends,
my *Baltimore Sun* friends, my neighborhood friends, my
mom friends, my author friends, my reader friends, my
New York friends, my New Orleans friends, my Facebook
friends, my Twitter friends.

I am tired of the literal deaths and the figurative
deaths, the growing number of people I have to mourn.
Rob's Facebook account remains not only open but ac-
tive, a place to share memories of him. My friends who
lost their daughter continue to upload photographs of
her, which I find uncommonly generous. It's almost as
if they are comforting me, the writer who never has the
right words, the former reporter who never knows what
to ask.

It's all about you, isn't it, Laura?

To reiterate: I am well aware of everything that's
wrong with Facebook and Twitter. I have seen my friends
abused. I understand the misuse of our data, the ex-
tremities of cancel culture, the lack of nuance, the echo

chambers we create within our online communities. Inspired by my friend Andre Dubus III, I have stripped my smartphone, trying to make it as dumb as possible. When I'm out in the world I have no access to social media or games, and I try not to check email. The other day, I talked to a barista while waiting for my latte. It was lovely.

But at the end of the day, at the literal end of the goddamn day, when I'm often alone in a quiet house where my daughter sleeps, Facebook and Twitter have kept me company. If my personae on those platforms irritate those who know me well—and I've received some feedback that this is the case—then #sorrynotsorry. I've got a landline, I've got a mailbox. Feel free to use them anytime. Knock on my back door with a bottle of wine and I'll sit outside with you, talking late into the night.

I'm a shitty friend, no argument there. But there's still time, I hope, to be a better one.

Postscript: Immediately after finishing this essay, I threw myself into a huge decluttering project at home. On the mantel in the dining room, we keep an assortment of odd things—sticks from the graves of famous bluesmen, a piece of the Berlin wall, a bird nest, shells our daughter has gathered. Some of those items sit on a series of small tiles, gifts from my Charley friend. There are six in all. One is chipped and one is cracked clear in half. I guess the other four represent the friends who would help me bury a body.

I may be a shitty friend, but life is a shitty novelist.

Part II
This Be the Other Verse

*They didn't fuck me up,
my mom and dad. On that
score, I'm a self-made woman.*

My Father's Bar

I stole my father's bar. I never meant to. It began as a joke, and not even mine. I had recently joined the staff of the Baltimore *Evening Sun*, which was owned by the same company as *The Sun*, where my father had worked as an editorial writer for most of my life. I had landed my dream job in my dream city, Baltimore. (Don't scoff.) I was thirty and finding my way in the world. I needed a bar, my bar, in Baltimore, something a step up from the dives and icehouses of my twenties, a decade spent in Texas. I can't remember what the other Baltimore contenders were. Midtown Yacht Club, with peanuts on the floor? The Calvert House, a mere two blocks from *The Sun* building? I did love Alonso's, a dim place that didn't take credit cards and served a dish called the Fish Thing, but it was way up on the north side.

My father preferred the Brass Elephant, a gracious town house in the city's Mount Vernon neighborhood, just five blocks from *The Sun*. His drink of choice was a gin martini, although my father would stipulate—as will I—that "gin martini" is redundant. The only true martini is made from gin and dry vermouth, with just the tiniest whiff of the latter. Olives or lemon peels are okay, but why would you want to displace even a drop of gin with those foreign objects?

My father was famous for drinking martinis—and for giving them up, usually for a week or so at the beginning of a new year. "So Long, Lippman" was the headline on an op-ed column written by his good friend and fellow martini connoisseur G. Jefferson Price III. But Lippman always came back. More than one photograph was taken of my father and the last martini of the year; the best showed him in a snowy backyard in hat and scarf, holding the quite chilly martini aloft.

That said, I don't think I ever saw my father inebriated except once, on a Christmas Eve at my home, where my sister noticed there was a slight waver to his walk and asked if he was ill. "I'm fine," he said. "Just not used to that expensive gin Laura buys." My father swore by cheap gin, Beefeater, which he kept in the freezer. I think he was rather disappointed with my flirtations with Tanqueray and Hendrick's.

But that was later. In the fall of 1989, a colleague of my father's thought it would be hilarious if I was sitting at the bar at the Brass Elephant when my father arrived for an after-work drink to celebrate his sixtieth birthday. He did think it was funny. Sort of. Like many fathers of daughters, mine did not want me to embrace *all* the things he loved—newsrooms and martinis among them. He offered to pay my way through graduate school if I would choose any other profession. "I'm afraid newspaper work coarsens a woman," he said once when I used a profanity so mild that it could have slid past Standards and Practices on a network sitcom.

After seeing me with a martini at the Brass Elephant Bar, he went there less and less, while I went there more and more. It could have been a coincidence. He retired from the newspaper in 1995, lured by a generous buyout, began spending most of his time in the small Delaware beach town where my parents would eventually settle. The bar was mine.

The Brass Elephant was hushed and civilized, a grown-up bar for proper grown-ups, something I wanted to be when I was thirty. A quarter of a century later, I no longer remember why I was so anxious to be a grown-up. I bought my first house within a year of turning thirty. (My father advised against it.) Within three years, I would marry a man who loved the Brass Elephant as much as I did. My father paid for the tent that covered my back-yard. Within ten years, I would find myself lying to that same man, now a so-called househusband, pretending that I had to work later than necessary so I could go to the bar with a female friend instead of coming straight home, as he expected me to. Instructed me to.

When I started writing crime novels set in Baltimore, I gave the Brass Elephant to my series character. Private investigator Tess Monaghan was never more my proxy than when sitting at the Brass Elephant bar, the light from the setting sun slanting through the pink-and-green stained glass window, a plate of farfalle pasta or the divine mozzarella en carrozza in front of her. Eventually the bar created an eponymous drink in her honor; a menu from the party celebrating that drink hangs in my office. The drink had peach schnapps in it. I don't much care for schnapps and—now it can be told—I didn't love the drink, although it wasn't quite as bad as I had feared.

I can admit that now because the Brass Elephant closed in 2009. A new place has opened in the same spot, but I don't have the heart to go there. Because, in some ways, I don't want to be reminded of the young woman who used to climb the mahogany staircase to the second-floor bar, the woman who was in such a hurry to be a grown-up. I find it easier to romanticize the dives of my true youth, where the mistakes and stakes were smaller. The Brass Elephant, through no fault of its own, became the backdrop to a failed first marriage and a roller-coaster ride of a newspaper career. For even as my career as a novelist took off, my career as a reporter stalled, a crazy, sad story that no one really believes, so I've learned to stop telling it. My father worked at *The Sun* for thirty years and I set my goal at thirty-one, having landed there at a much younger age than he did. We were somewhat competitive, my father and I. At any rate, I lasted only twelve years at *The Sun*, which eventually swallowed the *Evening Sun*, twenty in newspapers overall.

I last visited the Brass Elephant in 2012, when I was writing a novel to be published in early 2014. I made it the hangout for a band of devoted John B. Anderson volunteers who repair there on Election Night to lick their wounds. A very young woman talks to the bartender, who remembers her father, a man who disappeared four years earlier to evade federal charges for running a gambling operation. The bartender claims to know what her father would have thought about the 1980 presidential election and the young woman yearns to believe him. She knows surprisingly little about her father.

I wish I had asked the bartender of my day more questions about my father. Because, while my father is still alive—and still enjoys a daily martini, just one, at which he nips off and on while watching *Law & Order* reruns—my father tells fewer and fewer stories. His memory is problematic. He's no longer quick, and my father was famously quick, an award-winning columnist who packed more in six hundred words than others could in fifteen hundred. Whenever I visit or call, the one thing he always asks is if I know any gossip from our old workplace. I don't. In a way, the *Baltimore Sun* is like another Brass Elephant. A newspaper is still published in the building, but it's not the newspaper I knew and certainly not the one for which my father worked, a sober, well-regarded place with foreign bureaus and, back in the day, a policy that required my father to travel first-class when covering presidential elections. While my father watches *Law & Order*, it is my mother and my husband who stalk his family tree, genealogical detectives on a case as cold as a martini straight from the shaker.

And I have said goodbye to the Brass Elephant, although poetic license would allow me to revive it in the pages of my books. I briefly aspired to finding a new bar—there's a cool, hipsterish place a block from my house—but the fifty-something self-employed writer requires much less watering than the thirty-something newspaper hack. I go to restaurant bars for lunch now—a ladylike salad, a glass of wine, never a martini. I had one at a steakhouse the other night and it was as if someone had slipped me a roofie; I fell asleep facedown on the sofa and could barely be roused to stumble into bed. I am only five years away from my own sixtieth birthday and I would prefer not to find my daughter sipping a martini anywhere on that celebratory day, given that she will be not quite nine at the time. I really hope she won't be a writer, although she has expressed some interest in what I do. The other day, I showed her a prize I had won. Her eyes brightened at the shiny, inexpensive object: "Can I have it?"

And although my father will probably not read this essay—he is reading less and less these days—it's as good a place as any to issue an apology for doing what children have always done and will always do when it comes to their parents' possessions and memories and lives.

Daddy, I'm sorry I stole your bar.

The Thirty-First Stocking

When my mother was twenty-one, maybe twenty-two, she bought a knitting kit at an Atlanta notions store. The kit had everything one needed to make a personalized Christmas stocking—a pattern, red, green, and white yarn; jingle bells; a small cloud of angora for Santa Claus's beard. Already a proficient knitter—argyle socks had been the rage during her high school years—she needed less than a week to make a stocking for her young cousin Peg.

Over the next five decades, she would make twenty-nine more stockings. For herself, for her new husband, Theo. For their first daughter, born in 1956. For the second daughter—me—born in 1959. A nephew, a niece. Family friends. My sister's husband. The nephew's wife. My first husband, although not my second. The kits were discontinued at some point, but my mother had kept the instructions and the pattern. Even when there was that long stocking-free stretch through the 1970s and into the '80s, she saved those instructions. Her friends began having grandchildren and the stockings started again.

Finally, in 2010, I could tell my mother that *she* was going to be a grandmother. Given that I was fifty-one, she had pretty much given up hope.

"Do you want me to make a stocking?" Of course I did.

But the thirty-first stocking turned out to be problematic from the start.

To begin with, there was the matter of the name. My husband and I had long agreed that, should we ever have a daughter, we would call her Georgia Rae. He told people we had chosen the name to honor Ray Charles and the song he had popularized, "Georgia on My Mind." I, ever more pedantic, explained we had appropriated the name from a singer-songwriter, John Hiatt. *He* had named his daughter for Ray Charles and then written a song about her; we were just copycats. But I liked the "Georgia" because it was a reference to the state where I was born, the state were most of my relatives still lived.

And what if it was a boy? I yearned to use some variation of my father's name, but my husband was adamant: No names for living people. That's Jewish law and he's a Jew, the kind of Jew who says things like: "The synagogue I fail to attend must be conservative." A Jew who eats bacon and shellfish and marries shiksas, but wants to raise his children as Jews. Upon our marriage, I readily agreed to that condition, although, unlike his previous wife, I didn't convert. I was a Protestant, the kind of Protestant who says things like: "I don't see the point of being non-observant in two religions."

But I did see the point of getting my own way, whenever possible. And I had covered politics quite a bit during my twenty-year newspaper career; I knew how consensus was made, how to build alliances. I waylaid my stepson, already a talented jazz pianist as a teenager, and brokered a deal: I would let him name his future baby brother Thelonious, as long as the boy was called Theo. He said he would throw his support behind me if the middle name was Parker, for another one of his jazz heroes. Done! We presented the name to his father, a fait accompli. Thelonious Parker Simon, Theo for short.

We planned to shorten the girl's name as well, calling

her Rae. But when she showed up in May 2010, she was so clearly a girl meant to be called Georgia Rae. As the John Hiatt song begins: "I know a girl, mess with your mind." Boy, did she. The force of her personality was evident before she was twenty-four hours old. She was born the night of a full moon, part of a bumper crop of babies. Twenty-two children were delivered in the hospital that night. We like to say that only eighteen went home with personalities, that Georgia Rae had crept from bed to bed, sucking the life force out of at least three.

But if Georgia Rae was big enough to handle her name, her stocking was not. At least, that is the story my mother tells now, making excuses for the truncated RAE at the top of the thirty-first stocking. Ever gallant, she claims that she chose to use only the second name because Georgia Rae didn't fit. I never point out that she made a stocking for her niece, Elizabeth, whose name is only one letter shorter, or that she has a stocking in her own name, Madeline. She is, as she is inclined to do, letting me off the hook. I was the one who told her to make the stocking for "Rae." It was the first time my daughter put me on notice that she would decide who she was, how she would be known. It would not be the last.

Still, I looked forward to filling that misnamed stocking. In my childhood, stocking gifts were often the best thing about Christmas Day, the true surprises, things not found on any list. A painted box with a unicorn on its cover—that was from my mom. A brass monkey that functioned as a cardholder. "I just thought it looked like something you would love," said my first husband, and he was right. Things like that. I knew our daughter, not quite seven months old on Christmas Day, would have little use for whatever came out of her stocking on that first Christmas, but one day—oh wait, she was going to be raised a Jew. Well, her brother, who had been raised a Jew by a woman who had gone to the trouble of converting, had still enjoyed all the Christmas rituals. There was no reason that Georgia Rae could not.

But first she had to become a Jew, officially. The daughter of a non-Jewish woman is not a Jew, not until she's taken a mikvah, the ritual bath. Been dunked, in my husband's vernacular. Shades of Achilles, she would have to be completely immersed as rabbis gave a blessing. And in order for our daughter to be dunked, we had to pass a test of sorts.

On a bitter-cold day in early December, we drove to a

synagogue in Washington, D.C., and sat before a panel of three rabbis, including the one who officiated at my stepson's bar mitzvah. There was bad blood between this rabbi and me, although she didn't know it. She had prohibited me from being on the bimah during my stepson's bar mitzvah because I am not a Jew. Other non-Jews were up there that day, but she didn't realize that, so she didn't ban them. My husband wishes I would stop bringing this up. He points out that I could have participated during a part of the service when the Torah was not open. He believes the rabbi acted appropriately. I think she was trying to shake my husband down because he didn't have an official "get"—the document that Jewish husbands are obligated to present during a divorce. At any rate, I was still holding that grudge three years later.

But on this particular day, I was a supplicant. So I behaved very well, facing that panel of three rabbis. I explained that I had chosen not to convert, but I would do everything I could to help my husband raise our daughter as a Jew. (*Not in your synagogue*, I thought of my rabbi-nemesis.) After all, I had done that for my stepson—driving him to Hebrew school and, well, driving him home from Hebrew school.

What about Christmas? one of the rabbis asked me.

Oh yeah. Christmas. What about it? I had not put up a Christmas tree or hung my stocking since my husband and I began living together eight years earlier. Christmas decorations really bugged him and I had discovered that I didn't miss them at all. No more pine needles to vacuum. We exchanged gifts on December 25 and then, in the great Jewish tradition, went to the movies and ate Chinese food. I had experience celebrating Christmas this way. As it happens, my first husband was born on Christmas Day and I had always tried to make December 25 about him, not the holiday. So we went to the movies and ate Chinese food. Christmas really wasn't that important to me. Besides, this wasn't a legally binding conversation. I could do whatever I wanted once I left that synagogue.

"We will not observe Christmas in our household," I told the rabbis in a sudden burst of inspiration. "I will pack up her stocking, the ornaments I own, and take them to my sister's house. We will explain Christmas to her as a practice observed by others, but not us. I don't believe that people should cherry-pick religions for the best parts. You have to choose one and stick with it."

We passed the test and descended to the basement, where there was a small round pool, no different from any health club Jacuzzi, to my eyes. My husband, in a bathing suit, took hold of our naked child and pulled her under the water in one quick swoosh, making sure not to miss a patch of skin. When they surfaced, she looked furious, on the verge of a vengeful scream. But then the rabbis began to sing and she was distracted by the Hebrew syllables bouncing off the tiles in the steamy air. It was beautiful.

On the drive home, I all but cackled at how slick I had been in front of the rabbis. I told the story over and over to the family that gathered that night to celebrate. *I was going to give up Christmas! I was going to take all the ornaments to my sister's house!* I was like the French knight in *Monty Python and the Holy Grail*, sniggering at King Arthur and his knights in their futile quest. "I tol' them we've already got one!"

Lies have a strange way of making themselves true. Less than two weeks later, I packed up all the Christmas things in my household and took them to my sister's. The thirty-first stocking was not hung that year. Almost four years later, it has yet to be hung. We go to my sister's house on Christmas Eve, but the things I gave her remain boxed. Maybe this year, now that Georgia Rae is more aware, we will let her have a stocking over there. Last year, contemplating the Christmas season's riches, she moaned to me: "I wish I weren't Jewish." She asked for lights on the house, but my husband could not bear it, not even in Hanukkah-friendly blue and white. It turns out that he is also the kind of Jew who would be ashamed—his word—if another Jew came to his home in December and saw lights in any color or configuration. We compromised and began hanging lights during Mardi Gras season, in strings of purple, green, and gold. We tell people that's our true religion, anyway. Secular humanist Mardi Gras–ism with a side of voodoo.

Meanwhile, I kept my promise to the rabbis, trying to help my husband raise our daughter as a Jew. I learned to make challah. I bought a kiddush cup. I made latkes for Hanukkah. I hosted Passover, although I had it catered. When my husband had to travel for work, I downloaded prayers from the Internet, threw a napkin on my head, and, sneaking a peek through my eyelashes, recited the words phonetically. *Baruch atah adonai . . .* Losing Christmas was easy.

I hadn't counted on losing God, too.

NOW, IF YOU had asked me five years ago to define my religious beliefs, I would have leaned hard on the word "Deist." I had been brought up as a Presbyterian, a word often used as a slur by my husband and in-laws, a way of connoting someone prissy or bland, someone who eats a bagel with butter on it. (I have never eaten a bagel with butter on it.) I went to church through the age of twelve, then stopped, a decision my parents supported. I came to believe there was a central intelligence to the universe, but accepted that it was so multidimensional that I could never understand it. This power did not, as I understood it, respond to petitionary prayer. But there was no harm in speaking to God, trying to sort things out. I had been talking to God all my life, since I was four or five. As a child, I imagined a man in a blue robe and a black crew cut, leaning over a cloud, his arms open as if to embrace me. *Are you there, God, it's me, Laura.* I talked to God more often than anyone knew. I made promises, most of which I broke. (At the age of twelve, reeling from a suicide attempt by someone close to me, I told him I would give up Peanut M&M's if the person lived.) Yet I believed in him.

Then, one day, I found I could no longer justify this belief. It didn't happen in a flash. But things started to unravel in front of the rabbis, when I blithely said: "I don't believe that people should cherry-pick religions for the best parts." Wasn't I cherry-picking? I didn't believe in hell. Heck, I didn't believe in any afterlife, much as I yearned to. I was skeptical of all organized faiths. I couldn't embrace any aspect of religion that seemed to exist only to reward belief. Yet—I had believed in God and now I didn't. It was hard. It's still hard. If someone asked me point-blank how I define myself, I would probably say that I'm an atheist who yearns to be proven wrong. Not because I want an afterlife. Not because I fear hell. I want there to be a God because I really miss talking to him.

In that way, God is not unlike my first husband, the Christmas Day baby whose stocking also was put away, many years ago, and remains in an unmarked box somewhere in my basement. What number was that? The twenty-third or the twenty-fourth? It's easy to lose count.

But that was the first stocking to be retired, strictly speaking. Everyone for whom my mother has made a stocking is still alive as far as I know. Meanwhile, my mother's friends are having great-grandchildren now. A thirty-second stocking seems possible, maybe a thirty-third.

But the stockings can't go on forever. Nothing does. One day, the stockings will end and I won't even have my crew cut God for comfort. Still, I have kept my word to the rabbis, and there is honor in that. Atheists, who have no one to make rules for us, have to figure out right and wrong for ourselves. I tell my daughter that our household has one inviolate rule: Keep your promises, don't ever lie.

Luckily, the rabbis didn't think to ask me about Easter.

Swing, Interrupted

I have no natural athletic ability, although I have always looked as if I might—tall, broad-shouldered, with muscular arms and legs. I run slowly, with an awkward gait. To say that I throw like a girl is unfair to girls everywhere. P.E. class, to me, was something created to jeopardize my precious 4.0 grade-point average. (I managed to eke out an A-minus, thanks to written tests and the credit given merely for showing up and suiting up, which turned out to be a pretty useful life lesson.) I swam well enough to be a lifeguard, but not swiftly enough to be part of Baltimore's ubiquitous swim team culture. I learned to ice-skate, but only after two miserable years of walking on my ankles. We had a word for kids like me in the 1970s, a decidedly non-P.C. one, derived from the term "spasmodic." I heard that word a lot.

But when I was fourteen, I joined my mother for a tennis lesson and it looked, ever so briefly, as if I might have found a sport for which I had some aptitude. For a couple of weeks, we met with an instructor at the public courts near our house. The plan was for us to take lessons together, play together, improve together. Then my father put a stop to it. I was in an accelerated program at school that had a reputation for being difficult. He wanted me to focus on my studies. My mother continued her tennis lessons; her skills quickly outpaced mine, and she found a new partner.

For the next forty-plus years, I tried to play tennis off and on, but it was a frustrating experience, marked by what my first husband taught me to call the yips—a jittery mental state that made it impossible for me to execute the simplest strokes on a reliable basis. My forehand was awful. Nine times out of ten, I either lofted the ball way too high, or hit it into the bottom of the net.

Flash-forward to the summer of 2018: I decided my young daughter should take weekly tennis lessons with two sets of siblings. None of our kids seemed to have any particular talent for tennis, but I enjoyed the company of the other moms. And I found myself yearning to pick up a racket again and see if I could unlock the tennis player I suspected was inside me. My father, dead for three years, was no longer calling the shots. Instead of wondering what might have been, I could find out what would be.

I convinced one of the other moms that we should take lessons when our kids went back to school. Still, it seemed unlikely that I could take on a new physical venture at the age of fifty-nine. Muscle memory is real and most of my muscles have no memories. But six months later, barely a week has gone by when I have failed to play tennis. I'm still not athletic, but I'm strong. I've been working out with a trainer for almost fifteen years. I walk or bike to run most errands. And as I'd suspected, some skills were still there—a two-handed backhand, a natural instinct for volleying, and a dogged competitiveness that makes me run *for everything*. "Great get," my instructor says frequently. Mostly I hear: "Hit the ball all the way through, *allllllllllll* the way through." My forehand thuds, thuds, thuds into the net, or soars embarrassingly high into the sky. Sometimes I want to stamp my feet in frustration. But I don't. I just keep trying. If writing novels has taught me anything, it's that progress isn't linear.

So I persevere. I am a terribly competitive person. (That adjective is chosen with precision. I care about winning and it's terrible.) This is my father's legacy; he loved to win. After decades of playing poker, he decided to stop, declaring with uncharacteristic self-knowledge: "I mourned a dollar lost more than I ever celebrated a dollar won." My father was the competitor I faced most often. In checkers, gin rummy, Parcheesi, dominoes, and, sometimes, tennis. An indifferent, not particularly skilled player, he always rose to the occasion when I was on the other side of the net. He beat me like a drum, sometimes singing a taunting tune to boot. He wanted to be the kind of parent who could lose gracefully, maybe even intentionally, to his child. But once the game was afoot, he wanted to win.

When I was eight, he decided to teach me an important lesson about gambling. I needed $2 to buy a Sonny & Cher album from Korvette's. (I think that sentence has more anachronisms per character count than any sentence ever written.) He asked if I was willing to bet the money I had saved by playing the No Game. All I had to do was answer no to every question asked. How hard could that be? Such a simple game. Just say *no*.

"Are you ready to play, do you understand the rules?"

I narrowed my eyes and shouted: "NO!"

He sputtered with surprise, outraged and proud.

Who would I be if my father had allowed me to take tennis lessons? I have a great life; I'm not worried about some existential tennis pro road not taken. But the *yips*. All this time, I have remained a choker par excellence. Once, at a bowling competition between two teams of crime novelists, I clinched the game with a spare. "Ah, but did you know you needed to get that many pins?" asked my now-husband. He knows me too well. I won the game for my team only because I had no idea that the onus was on me to do just that. That's why the worst part of tennis class is the last ten minutes, when our instructor makes us play mock points. My friend is fifteen years younger, with a formidable serve and smash. I suspect that she, too, will outgrow me as my mother did. She wins more points. She maintains that she's not a superior athlete and that she can't envision a day she won't want to hit with me. And maybe that's true because I think we both prefer to stand on the baseline and rally to one another, aiming to keep the ball in play as long as possible. It's not about winners and losers, even though it's my genetic birthright to think in those terms.

The rap on my father is that he was an indulged only child who never learned to lose. He had the best intentions. He would start a game of checkers, spot me four pieces, and, inevitably, find himself about to be defeated. So he would point to something behind me—"What's that in the corner?"—knock over the board with his knee, and blame our Scottish terrier.

What will the rap on me be when my daughter is grown? I try to model the behavior of a good sport, but I feel this insistent desire to win—and an equal desire to hide the compulsion. I wouldn't want the world to know what goes through my mind during a game of Go Fish. But in the end, I am happy—truly happy—to lose to my daughter, who has a staggering confidence I can only envy. "I'm pretty much better at everything than you are, Mom," she says, and I agree. Although she conceded, after watching me on the court recently, that I seemed to be making steady progress at tennis.

After a recent class, I said to the instructor: "My forehand is in my head—and it needs to find its way to my arm." He agreed, but seemed confident that at some point my arm would learn what my head knows. I'm not so sure. Still, I take the lessons to confront that part of me that balks, that would rather lose fast than risk a drawn-out defeat. If a point does go on? The odds that I win it seem to go up, mostly because I dive for strategic-but-ugly shots. I hate myself for those graceless shots, but I make them, ever prepared to sacrifice form for triumph. And then there are moments when I miss forehands so easy that our instructor, who usually alternates shots to my friend and me, hits another one to me. And then another one, and another one, and another one. He never says a negative word.

My brain yells at my arm: "Could you please take over?"

My arm replies: "Maybe one day, lady, but you still have a lot of work to do on yourself."

Revered Ware

Four to five times a week, I reach into the cabinet to the left of my stove and pull out my ugliest, least-pedigreed pan. Actually, it's two pans: a double boiler. The bottom is scuffed and darkened from decades of use; the insert, which is never meant to come directly in contact with heat, has swollen because someone who prefers not to be named put it directly on the burner.

No one else seems to consider a double boiler an essential piece of equipment. You won't find it on the lists compiled by even the most down-to-earth food writers. I can't recall the last time I saw one mentioned in a recipe. Yet it's essential to me, because I'm a work-at-home writer who likes to reheat leftovers for lunch and make brownies on the spur of the moment. (Every work-at-home writer needs a way to procrastinate; mine is baking, although cleaning the baseboards with a Q-tip will also do in a pinch.)

Reheating leftovers in a double boiler produces a superior, if slower, result when compared with food heated in a microwave. I have met people who want to argue this point, who claim that my taste buds couldn't possibly tell the difference, but you don't actually need a great palate to find the dead, cold spots in leftovers that have been microwaved. And while a double boiler takes longer, it requires virtually no oversight. It's hard to burn something—unless, ahem, you put the insert directly on an open flame.

Yet the thing I most appreciate is that a double boiler is *not* a microwave. I hate microwaves. I didn't grow up with one, and I'm not going to grow old with one. In that way, I am channeling my late father, who was highly skeptical of many things.

A hypochondriac, my father often played his many worries for laughs, but they were real. He worried about jaundice. (His feet would turn yellow from wearing loafers without socks.) He worried about cholesterol. He worried about skin cancer—justifiably, as it turned out. He worried that his beloved martinis would lead to a fatty liver. He quit them on a regular basis, usually at year's end; they always reunited by Valentine's Day.

Most of all, my father worried about radiation. He ordered my sister and me to sit ten feet from our black-and-white television. He fought the dentist over X-rays, instructing his daughters to do the same. The most famous story about my father's anti-radiation stance involved a waterproof watch, a Christmas gift. Toweling off after a shower, he recalled reading that luminous watch dials might emit radiation. He had to know immediately if his new watch glowed in the dark. But it was a weekday morning, bright and sunny. He tried to check the dial while standing in his closet, but the door would not latch. He went into my mother's closet. The good news was that his watch did not shine. The bad news was that the closet door had locked behind him and there was no one else in the house. A cleaning lady would arrive soon. Bad news: He would have to greet her naked or wearing his wife's clothes. *Naked or in a dress, naked or in a dress, naked or in a dress?* My father, born in 1929, was an exceedingly modest man. He kicked the door down.

When microwaves became ubiquitous in the 1970s, it

was understood that the Lippman household would continue to make stovetop popcorn. Do microwaves release harmful radiation? Only if they're improperly sealed or leaking, according to the Food and Drug Administration. But I don't actually care anymore.

None of the things my father feared—radiation, cancer—killed him; he died after a sudden stroke in 2014. The death of an eighty-five-year-old man who has suffered two falls in less than twelve months can never be said to be unexpected, but what happened next was: I took over his neuroses the way I took the never-worn socks my mother had knitted for him a few weeks before his death.

When airport travel, a big part of my life, requires me to use the screening booths, I now request pat-downs, knowing full well I will be exposed to more radiation on the flight. At the dentist, I am perversely proud when I glimpse my dental chart: *Refused X-rays*. I would probably worry about my cell phone if my father had ever owned one, but that technology never became part of his life. Doesn't everyone do this? Assume a habit or an everyday item that keeps a loved one close? My father's quirks are my inheritance, the way I keep his memory alive.

I never use my double boiler without thinking about him. I even like to use it to make popcorn as he taught me—just the bottom part, three "testers" in a tablespoon of oil, then a half cup of kernels, shaking the covered pan constantly, letting a little steam escape, bringing the heat down steadily, removing the pan as soon as there's a long lull between pops. My popcorn has been eerily perfect as of late: no hulls, no burned bits. What I don't know is if I love all double boilers as much as I love this one in particular. Although neither my sister nor my mother can confirm it, I believe that mine is the cast-off double boiler bequeathed to me when I moved into my first apartment, one that has now moved with me eight times over forty years. A cheap thing, a pot no one would envy. But if I'm right, then the handle I hold as I shake the popcorn is one my father held, too.

I'm just going to say that I'm right.

Part III
My Life as a Villainess

I'm not bad, I just draw myself that way.

The Waco Kid

1.

People sometimes ask how I ended up in Waco, Texas, for my first job out of college. I don't like to brag, but it was the result of a careful, methodical campaign in which I spent six months trying to find a newspaper gig in New England.

I graduated from Northwestern University's Medill School of Journalism in 1981. The economy was not in great shape in general and journalism jobs in particular were hard to find. And although Medill had cheerfully taken my parents' cash money for four years, its placement office had no interest in placing me anywhere, except, perhaps, a fifth year in Medill. The school's official line was that the journalism education wasn't complete unless one stayed for graduate school.

I wanted *out*. I loved Northwestern, but Medill was a snake pit, a cruel place that reveled in its cruelty. The faculty claimed they were preparing us for the real world, which they swore would be far worse, assuming we could even find a foothold there. Post-Watergate, we were told, there were so many would-be reporters in the country's journalism schools that if every single working journalist died the next day, there still wouldn't be enough jobs for all the people studying journalism.

And that was day one, at orientation. It only got worse from there. By my senior year, I felt as if I had spent four years running a gauntlet of Mean Old White Men. (There was one outstanding exception, Sallie Gaines, a *Chicago Tribune* copy editor who treated her students with love and respect.)

In the early 1980s, applying for newspaper jobs, absent a connection, meant sending a cover letter, résumé, and clips to managing editors. My father was in the business, but I had shockingly few connections. An editor at the *Chicago Sun-Times* agreed to see me, but he had no encouraging words. *Chicago Tribune* columnist Bob Greene suggested we meet for lunch and talk about my future. Surprise, surprise, lunch was switched to dinner and he wasn't interested in my future beyond that evening. (I walked out.)

Meanwhile, all those letters to New England towns—Fall River, Bedford, Bennington, Manchester, Plymouth, Salem—they all went unacknowledged.

I had one tiny ace up my sleeve, an internship I had completed at the *Atlanta Constitution*, the biggest newspaper in the Cox chain. My Atlanta supervisor told me that one of the Cox sister papers, the *Waco Tribune-Herald*, was looking for reporters, and its editor-in-chief had worked in Atlanta.

The *Tribune-Herald's* interest was gratifyingly immediate. I looked good on paper, I was told. Problem was, my paper profile wasn't sufficient. They didn't hire without a face-to-face interview and they didn't pay anyone's travel expenses for such interviews.

I took a twenty-eight-hour Greyhound bus from Chicago to Waco, changing twice, in St. Louis and Dallas. I left Chicago on Wednesday afternoon, arrived in Waco after dark on Thursday. I went to the only motel within walking distance of the bus station; it was exactly what you would expect from a motel within walking distance of the Greyhound bus station in Waco, Texas.

On Friday, I was interviewed by four editors, all white men, at least three of whom told me that Waco was the buckle on the Bible Belt and a great place to raise a family. They offered me a job before I left. I told them I would like to think about it and got back on the bus. But I knew I was going to take the job. It was the only offer I had.

My starting salary was $175 a week, not quite $500 in today's dollars. Back at Northwestern, my news photography instructor, Howard Finberg, mocked my gig, called me the Waco Kid, the name of the alcoholic sharpshooter that Gene Wilder plays in *Blazing Saddles*. My parents had paid thousands of dollars for me to go to Northwestern, Northwestern had done nothing to help me get a job, and now my instructor was making fun of me.

That was Medill in a nutshell. That was why I had to get out. If that meant becoming the Waco Kid, so be it.

2.

I arrived in Waco after two days on the road, driving a Ford Escort that was packed to the brim and had a fake

woman, known as Aunt Bea, strapped into the front pas-
senger seat. (My roommates and I had fashioned this
"artwork" for our apartment living room because, well,
we could. In her flowery dress and pink straw hat, she re-
sembled the character on *The Andy Griffith Show*.) I had
rented my apartment via phone. It was exactly what you
would expect from a Waco apartment rented via phone.
It had a burnt orange accent wall and cost $220 a month,
more than a third of my take-home pay. I headed straight
to Kmart to buy a few essentials.

There was a coin-operated "bucking bronco" outside
the Kmart, just like the ones I had ridden in my childhood.
A little girl was struggling with it. My heart soared—how
quaint, how lovely. Maybe I could be happy here.

To the best of my memory, it was June 22, a Monday.
On June 19, at a park two counties over, there had been a
huge Juneteenth celebration. "Juneteeth" marks the 1865
date when a Union officer, arriving in Galveston, brought
news that the slaves were free. In 1981, Juneteenth was
not well known outside Texas; a search of the *New York
Times* database from 1885 through 1980 doesn't yield a
single reference.

At the celebration in Limestone County, three African

American teenagers were arrested for possession of marijuana and pills on an island in the park's lake. Three deputies—two white, one black—decided to transport the young men by boat. The boat capsized thirty or forty feet from shore. Two deputies swam to safety. A third clung to the boat "like a spider," according to one eyewitness. All three teenagers drowned.

Given that that the deaths happened late Friday, the story would have first been reported in the *Waco Tribune-Herald* on Sunday, June 21. On Monday, it understandably continued to dominate page one. I'm a Southern native who has spent enough time in the North to know that no region is free of bigotry. But this was a daunting introduction to my new town. That little girl outside Kmart was the only thing giving me hope.

As I approached the store's front doors, I realized the girl was kicking the mechanical horse and screaming: "Give me back my money, you n——."

3.

Waco is different now, of course. Aren't we all? Haven't we all grown and changed since 1981?

When I got there, Waco was best known as the birthplace of Dr Pepper and the home of Baylor University. In 1993, its reputation would become entwined with the deadly Branch Davidian standoff, although locals would like you to know that this didn't happen within the town limits. And while Baylor has had quite the sexual assault scandal over the past few years, Waco is now Gainesville, as in Chip and Joanna Gaines, the married cohosts of HGTV's *Fixer Upper*, which went off the air in 2018 and is still available through Hulu and endless repeats. This extremely wholesome show has spawned a sprawling empire for the Gaineses—and a tourist boom for Waco.

But Waco, which likes to call itself the Heart of Texas, has a darkness it will never quite shake. New residents such as myself quickly learn about the 1953 tornado, one of the deadliest in Texas history. It struck downtown in the afternoon, killing 114 and injuring more than 600. Three decades later, when I walked the sad pedestrian mall that had failed to revive Waco's downtown, the tornado was still the official town bogeyman. But I sensed others lurking.

In the nineteenth century, Waco was known for its

lawlessness. William Cowper Brann, editor of the *Icono-clast* newspaper, is said to have divided the community with his diatribes against Baylor and the Baptists. (To be fair, he hated Episcopalians, too.) He was shot on April 1, 1898, and died of his injuries—but not before he managed to return fire and kill his assailant. Brann was such a divisive figure that his tombstone was vandalized repeatedly, and then stolen outright in 2009.

In the twentieth century, the city sought to remake its image, shed its Wild West reputation, even as its county, McLennan, racked up a shockingly high number of lynchings, fifteen overall, placing it second among Texas's 254 counties.

One specific vigilante-torture-death-by-mob—there really are no synonyms for "lynching"—received so much attention that it's said to have helped turn public attention against the practice. W. E. B. DuBois, then the head of the NAACP, devoted eight pages to the 1916 death of Jesse Washington in the *Crisis*, a new magazine. "The Waco Horror," as DuBois dubbed it, is considered seminal in changing the tide of public opinion, at least on the editorial pages of faraway newspapers. To be clear, lynchings continued for almost another seventy years in the United States, and not just in the South. But the Waco Horror helped to change the conversation.

No one ever spoke of the Waco Horror to me in the two years I lived there. The buckle on the Bible Belt cinched its waist tight, and good luck to those who didn't fit.

When I was in Waco, I often felt like Isadora Wing, the autobiographical heroine of Erica Jong's *Fear of Flying*, albeit with a less robust sex life. In the novel, Wing is living in Germany, where her second husband is stationed as a military doctor in the 1960s. She finds books in the local library with pro-Nazi sentiments and photographs that have been papered over. When she tells her therapist about her discoveries, he asks her why she's determined to publish an article about her findings. She says she is horrified by the hypocrisy, that she wants to tell the truth. The truth, her psychiatrist says, is that the Germans loved Hitler. Does she want to hear that?

Like Isadora Wing, I wanted to steam off the blank pages, expose Waco's darker side. I yearned to shock and provoke. A colleague and I wrote a first-person piece about how two "Yankees" adjusted to life in Waco; our editors were delighted with the hate mail it generated. As part of a film panel at Baylor, I described the *Porky's* movies, an R-rated franchise about sex-crazed high school boys, as "Andy Hardy with a hard-on," upsetting several coeds, who complained about my potty mouth. An anonymous caller threatened to harm me because of a film review in which I did not condemn interracial relationships; that marked the last time in my life I had a listed telephone number.

I remained oblivious to the dissonance in my own life, the things I had papered over, the hypocrisies and lies I allowed myself in heaping doses.

4.

From the moment I crossed the Brazos River and entered Waco, I was scheming to get out. It took twenty-six months and felt like forever. Yet when I look back, I'm struck by how much fun I managed to have, by how many things from Waco I've carried, literally and figuratively, across the decades. I got a lot of anecdotes out of Waco, and writers are suckers for anecdotes.

I acquired even more stuff, much of which I still own, most of it from flea markets and yard sales: a hall tree; an antique mirror; two salad bowls; a metal Suncrest orange soda thermometer; Fiestaware; a drop-leaf table; a set of dining room chairs; a $15 homemade rocking chair from a stand at Richland Mall. Most of the furniture had to be refinished, a task I chose to do inches from an old-fashioned gas heater in the living room of my second apartment. Honestly, I'm surprised I lived to tell the tale.

The other stories I have lived to tell include: The night my cat caught on fire while sitting next to a candle. (He was fine). Going on a rattlesnake roundup with a man named Butch and helping him catch seventeen snakes, by which I mean I stood nervously on a rock in my new-ish cowboy boots and said quietly, "I think I see one over there." Falling in love with a San Antonio man, also a reporter, who wanted to steer his car with his knees while playing harmonica.

I covered two different cases of matricide in nearby counties. In yet another homicide trial, I watched a man acquitted of all charges despite admitting that he hid behind a tree and took aim at the head of his wife's former lover. I chased the jury foreman from the courtroom, baffled; how had they failed to return at least a verdict of criminally negligent homicide against the man, based on his testimony? "We just don't think the DA made his case," the foreman told me.

One of my specialties was interviewing evangelists: a former heroin dealer who scared Sunday school classes straight; Rick Stanley, famous for being Elvis Presley's stepbrother; Lester Roloff, who ran a notorious "school" for boys. When I tried to ask Roloff a follow-up question about school prayer, he took my hand in his, stared into my eyes, and asked: "Laura, are you a Jew?"

I wasn't, only the granddaughter of one, but I put the Star of David on my checks when a woman at the local bank insisted I choose a design for my checkbook. "You gotta have something cute," she kept saying. "It's free!" The only person who ever noticed was the Jewish émigré who ran the gourmet food shop near my house.

5.

I fell in love with movies, driving regularly to Dallas (ninety miles) or to Austin (a hundred miles) to watch old films at revival houses. I subscribed to *Film Comment* and began studying for the GRE, thinking I might enter the film school at UT-Austin, take advantage of that sweet in-state tuition. I jumped at the opportunity to be the newspaper's second-string movie critic, especially when the entertainment editor told me I could expense two tickets even if I went the movies alone, because I wouldn't be paid for the reviews themselves. That was an extra $5!

Money was an issue, always. It immediately became apparent I couldn't afford $220 in rent, so I moved to a cheaper, funkier place, the one with the gas heater. For the first six months, before my pay was raised to $200 weekly, I waited tables at a local Italian restaurant, sometimes serving my bosses' wives. I once bought a twenty-five-pound sack of flour because it was so much cheaper by the pound than a five-pound sack. Mites got to it before I was three pounds in.

When I learned I needed my wisdom teeth removed, I shopped for the cheapest dentist in town. (I had health insurance, but no dental coverage.) I opted for a doctor who charged me $40 per tooth over three visits without anything more than Novocain. On the second visit, the tooth's root was more twisted than the X-ray indicated. This was before AIDS, or at least before anyone in Waco dentistry took precautions to avoid HIV infection, and by the time that tooth was out, the doctor was splattered with my blood and his toupee was askew. On the third and final visit, I burst into tears upon sitting down in the chair; he gave me a little laughing gas for free.

But I don't think my lack of funds was the reason I began to open packages of candy in the supermarket and eat a few pieces, then push the bags back to the rear of the shelf. Brach's chocolate-covered peanuts, M&M's, any kind of chocolate that wasn't double-wrapped. Because a bag of candy could be fortuitously open and anyone would help herself, that was just normal.

Whereas only someone with a *real* problem would open a bag and then unwrap a miniature candy bar.

6.

I was on a state highway west of Waco, heading to an interview, when I heard that Karen Carpenter had died. I've forgotten so much about my life, but I can summon up that scene, that precise moment. It was an overcast February day in Central Texas. I was probably thinking about my love life. I was forever thinking about my love life. My San Antonio boyfriend and I had started discussing whether to strike out for a new city where we might live together. Within weeks, he would tell me that he had decided to move to Guatemala and I cried into my chicken-fried steak, which happened to be the first solid food I had eaten in days. (I was in the middle of my wisdom teeth extraction.) But on that particular February day, we were still considering moving in together and I'm sure that was on my mind.

Karen Carpenter, dead. I hadn't thought about her in ages. I was much too cool for Karen Carpenter, whose records had been my soundtrack in junior high. My tastes had migrated to punk and New Wave and, because of my San Antonio boyfriend, lots of blues and jazz and conjunto. Initial news reports noted Carpenter had suffered from anorexia, but believed herself cured. It was several days before anorexia was listed as the cause of her heart failure.

This was what an eating disorder looked like to most people in the early 1980s—an extreme case of anorexia nervosa, like the one in the book and the TV movie *The Best Little Girl in the World*. Bulimic practices were everywhere—I knew girls at college who vomited and took laxatives—but purging had not yet had its movie-of-the-week (*Kate's Secret*), much less been entered into the *DSM*. An eating disorder was life-threatening. Everything else was just, you know, a funny thing you did sometimes, another anecdote. Almost every woman I knew made the same joke at least once: *If only I could be anorexic for just a little while.*

Years passed before I realized that although I never crossed the line into a full-out disorder, I was pretty screwed up about food. At the time, I would have simply told you I was hungry. I was always hungry, forever hungry.

The bottomless feeling had started in college. There could never be enough food. I wanted pizza and burgers and pancakes. I wanted endless bowls of vanilla pudding from the dorm dining room. I wanted peanut M&M's and chocolate-covered peanuts and Acme oatmeal chocolate chip cookies and hot fudge sundaes and frozen yogurt with salted peanuts. I didn't know what hunger was, so I didn't know what satiety was.

A good friend occasionally grabbed a grape or a cherry as we grocery-shopped. I was appalled. I don't think I registered the act as theft, merely as unusual, maybe unsanitary. The fruit hadn't been washed! *How could you?* I would ask my friend. Also—fruit, blech.

Yet not even two years later, I found myself wandering Waco's supermarkets after my evening shifts at the newspaper, opening bags of candy and sampling a piece or two, as if stolen chocolate didn't count. I'd then check out with my "healthy" choices. Pita bread? Yogurt? Cheese? When I was in my early twenties, I was firmly convinced that cheese was healthy and low-calorie.

One night after work, I indulged in my by-then-habitual foraging and headed to the checkout line. Someone tapped me on the shoulder. "I think you forgot something." I turned to see a man in a T-shirt and jeans, with a gun on his belt and a badge that he flashed at me. He also was strikingly good-looking, a Waco Tom Selleck. Yes, I was attracted to the cop who was busting me for stealing food.

Meekly, I took the open bag of Brach's chocolate-covered peanuts he pushed toward me. I didn't have enough cash to cover it along with my groceries, nor did I have a credit card. There were no POS terminals for ATM cards in 1981.

Luckily, I had a checkbook. I took out one of my Star-of-David-emblazoned checks and wrote the four digits required, probably somewhere between $10 and $15. Not even three hours earlier, I had been sitting in my cubbyhole at police headquarters, scanning the day's police reports for possible stories. If I hadn't had my checkbook, I could have ended up in the next day's police reports, accused of petty larceny.

I wish I could tell you that this incident solved everything. But that's not how things work. It would take almost thirty years for me to find some sanity where eating was concerned. The encounter did, however, put an end to what I now realize was a chronic shoplifting problem.

Of all the near-misses in Waco—refinishing furniture near the open flame of an old-fashioned gas heater, hunting for rattlesnakes, entrusting my wisdom tooth removal to Waco's cheapest dentist, falling in love—this is the one that I think about most often.

And it is the one story in my life I never told anyone, ever, not a boyfriend, not a husband, not even a therapist, until I wrote this piece.

7.

Waco is bigger now. Aren't we all? Yet I didn't see that coming. Oh, I knew the population had inched up, that there were new buildings, more development, in part because of the success of the various projects associated with *Fixer Upper*, such as the Magnolia Bakery and the Silos.

But when I took advantage of a Dallas business trip to visit Waco in November 2019, I was surprised by Waco's scale, how broad the streets are, how great the distances between locations. I was prepared for the changes, caught off guard by what remained the same.

I had no plan, just followed my instincts, driving east along Fourth Street, pretty sure that I would soon pass the police department where I once spent two nights a week, dutifully reading the police blotter. The building is now another city agency, but otherwise unchanged.

From there, I turned left on Waco Drive, heading south to see the two places where I once lived. The old duplex appears to have been converted back to a house; my first apartment, the one I couldn't afford on my $175 weekly salary, is terrifying. A recent makeover to the exterior, which seems to have been inspired by Joanna

Gaines's obsession with shiplap, didn't help. I drove north to the newspaper, reliving my old commute. The two-story red-brick building was larger than I recalled and I had completely blanked on the white columns that frame the front door. I turned south on Austin Street, found my way to the Kmart (gone) and Richland Mall.

It was when I turned into the mall parking lot that I figured it out—Waco is the generic town that has appeared and reappeared in my dreams off and on for almost forty years, a squat place in shades of greige beneath a huge and always overcast sky. These are not nightmares, just busy, mildly stressful episodes. I'm trying to get somewhere, but there are complications. Cars malfunction, I have to detour to pick people up and drop them off. Things aren't where they are supposed to be, but there is a river at the edge of town. The mall, Franklin Avenue, Waco Drive—they are all part of this familiar dreamscape.

It's common to project dislike on anyone, anything, with qualities that we dislike in ourselves. In Waco, I saw a place that wanted to be known for goodness—the Heart of Texas, the buckle on the Bible Belt—while disavowing its darkness. I pretended to be a good girl and I tried to be a cool girl, but I was neither. I was a boy-obsessed twenty-two-year-old who thought calories consumed while standing up in a grocery store didn't count, and that leaving a ruined bag of candy on a shelf wasn't stealing.

Waco was also a good foil. When you live in places where there is explicit racism and otherism, it's super-easy to feel great about yourself, to postpone some essential introspection. In my twenties, I believed that I could say and do certain things as long as I did it all with a kind of ironic self-awareness. I was wrong. Boy, was I wrong.

I circled downtown one more time, drove back down Waco Drive, almost got caught in the snarl of Sunday traffic outside the megachurch that occupies the site of the grocery store where I once bought a twenty-five-pound bag of flour to save a few bucks. I headed west on Twenty-Fifth Street, far seedier than I remember. I soon came to the old Safeway, boarded up. It appeared to have been vacant for quite some time. A sign on the plywood promised that a "Supermercado" would be coming soon.

Suddenly hungry, I tried to go to one of the local places I remembered with affection, Kim's or Vitek's, but neither kept Sunday hours. I settled for Taco Cabana, a Texas chain that I fell in love with in San Antonio, when

there was only one. My San Antonio boyfriend took me
there on my first visit in 1982 and instructed me that I
must eat a bean-and-cheese taco because it was the baseline, the taco by which all other tacos would then be
judged. At the Waco franchise, I ate a bean-and-cheese
taco in the near-empty restaurant—it was still prime
churchgoing hours—then headed back to Dallas.

8.

"Where you headed?" the Waco Kid asks Sheriff Bart at
the end of *Blazing Saddles*.

"Nowhere special."

"Nowhere special. I always did want to go there."

He saddles up, rides with the sheriff to the edge of
town—then gets in a limousine as the theme song swells.
*"He conquered fear and he conquered hate / he turned
our night into day . . ."* The song's not about him, but the
Waco Kid gets a happy ending just the same.

One Waco mystery followed me as I drove north on
I-35 to Dallas. After I left Waco in 1983, I returned several times over the next few years to visit my friends. At
some point, a stray bit of gossip was shared with me—

when my name came up, one of the top editors said I would never be forgiven for what had I done.

Wow—*never forgiven*. But what had I done? My furtive foraging remained a secret. Had he learned of the expense account I padded, those movie tickets added for my phantom companions so I might have an extra $5 here or there? But I had submitted those expenses with the entertainment editor's benediction, lagniappe for the time and labor I was essentially donating. Did he know I sometimes made personal long-distance phone calls at work? Had I forgotten to bring his wife extra rolls and butter when I waited on her during my moonlighting months? Whatever I had done, it must not have tainted me universally; the managing editor tried to hire me when he moved to another paper.

The editor with a grudge against me died in 2016, so I guess the story did, too. One day I'll be dead and all my grudges, earned and imagined, will go with me. That's how it works.

I was driving a Hertz "luxury" rental on that sunny November afternoon, a bright blue Chrysler 300, its radio tuned to a classic rock station that played Air Supply and Chicago, the sort of songs I would have tolerated on the company car's radio as I drove around Central Texas on assignment in the early '80s. I wasn't thinking about boys or food, my long-ago preoccupations. I was thinking about endings and how being the Waco Kid was probably one of the best things that had ever happened to me. I mulled how to end this story. I wanted wise words, profound words that would show how much I've grown and matured. I remembered Howard Finberg, the journalism prof who dubbed me the Waco Kid, something he probably doesn't even recall. Like Wally Wronken at the end of *Marjorie Morningstar*, I realized that the people at whom we yearn to thrust our successes don't really exist anymore. If you can't travel back in time and show them what you went on to accomplish, what's the point?

So I guess the only thing left to say is: Fuck you, Finberg.

Tweety Bird

1.

I was fifty-eight years old the first time I was called to the principal's office.

The summons came via email: "A few parents have forwarded to me the attached Twitter posts. These parents were concerned and they wanted to notify me of your posts."

My inner goody-goody, which I have never been able to vanquish, went into flight-or-flight mode. THE PRINCIPAL IS MAD AT ME. I AM IN TROUBLE! I HAVE TO GET OUT OF THIS. MUST AVOID CONFRONTATION AT ALL COSTS.

The principal even had screenshots of the tweet I had

sent three weeks earlier, which referenced a mean girl problem and my "solution." More than a thousand people had liked it, dozens of friends had commented favorably. The only negative reactions I saw were from two ladies in the Midwest, strangers to me, who thought I was threatening a child. The principal had screenshots of their scolding comments, too. The parents were concerned, the two Midwestern ladies were concerned, and now the principal said he, too, was concerned. Would I come to his office to discuss this?

I tried to get out of it. I argued that the tweet was ancient by social media standards. I fumed about my First Amendment rights. I was entitled to say what I wanted and the tweet was painstakingly composed to avoid identifying anyone. I asked if I should bring a lawyer. The principal said if I brought a lawyer, the school district would insist *he* have a lawyer. Did I really want to escalate things?

Finally, I caved and agreed to stop by the principal's office. "After my volunteering shift in her classroom if that's all right with you," I emailed pointedly. My daughter's school is a good one, within walking distance of our house, and—no small thing—free. She has had outstanding teachers so far. I like the parents I know. I like most of the kids, too.

But a few of the girls are, best I can tell, absolute bitches.

No, that's not what I tweeted.

2.

The telephone had "Mr. Watson, come here, I want to see you" or maybe it was "Mr. Watson come here I want you," there is some disagreement in the historical record. Twitter started on March 21, 2006, with Jack Dorsey typing—*tweeting*—"just setting up my twttr [sic]."

The name was inspired by Flickr, a photo-sharing app; the dropped vowels were part of a common strategy that helped secure domain names. Other potential names for this new SMS-based service included FriendStalker and Dodgeball. This suggests to me that Twitter's developers understood, at least subconsciously, the platform's potential for abuse. Why not just call it Dogpile and be done with it?

When I joined Twitter in 2010, it had about forty million users. Now its membership hovers at three hundred million. I know everything that is wrong with it. I know that trolls and bots target people for abuse and the site pretends it is helpless to stop it. I know that the users *are* the content, which means that writers are giving away their words for free. I know it is short on nuance and long on easy outrage. I wish tweets could be edited. I wasn't crazy about the 2017 decision to change the original character limit of 140 to 280.

I love it.

For a self-employed writer, Twitter is a water cooler, the company cafeteria, a barstool at a neighborhood tavern. I can sit "there" and say whatever occurs to me. And, sure, sometimes I do it while drinking.

I was not drinking when I wrote the tweet that got me sent to the principal's office. It was a blue-sky-perfect October afternoon and my husband had just returned from a field trip, the first he had chaperoned. He looked stricken. My husband spent a year embedded with the Baltimore city homicide squad, he has written about crime and war, prostitution and pornography. But nothing in his life had prepared him for the company of mean girls. Our daughter, taunted by one classmate in particular, had ended up crying on the field trip, prompting concerned parents to say helpfully to my husband, "Hey, your kid is crying." Now my husband seemed close to tears.

So I tweeted my mean girl revenge fantasy, which made my friends laugh because it was just that, a cathartic fantasy. A former reporter, I was careful in the tweet's construction. It was impossible to identify the girl—in a school of eight hundred kids, at least two hundred could have fit the description I crafted.

I think that's where the problem began.

3.

Were mean girls a thing before they were enshrined as *Mean Girls* in the 2004 film? The nonfiction book it was based on, *Queen Bees and Wannabes*, announced itself as a survival guide for the "new realities of girl world." I used to believe that creating the category made it aspirational. "Sometimes, I think I'm a mean girl," my own daughter has confessed to me. "Sometimes, I think I want to be."

But I'm the daughter of a children's librarian and when I consider the classic and not-so-classic books I read growing up, I realize that mean girls have always been with us. There are mean girls in *Little Women*, such as that horrible classmate who taunts Amy for not bringing a fashionable treat to school. Heck, there's Amy herself; she's definitely got the vibe. Laura, in the Little House books encounters the hateful Nellie Oleson by the third book in the series. Judy Blume's *Blubber* shows how quickly and arbitrarily girls can choose a victim.

But the single best book about mean girls is Eleanor Estes's *100 Dresses*, published in 1944. In Room 13 in a small-town school, Wanda Petronski is barely noticed, a quiet girl who wears the same faded blue dress every day. Outside the classroom, popular Peggy and her best friend Maddie like to "have some fun with her." They ask her, day after day, to recount how many dresses and pairs of shoes she has in her closet. Wanda insists she has a hundred dresses in a rainbow of hues.

"Peggy was not really cruel," Estes writes. "She protected small children from bullies. And she cried for hours if she saw an animal mistreated. If anybody had said to her, 'Don't you think that is a cruel way to treat Wanda?' she would have been surprised. Cruel? What did the girl want to go and say she had a hundred dresses for? Anybody could tell that was a lie. Why did she want to lie? And she wasn't just an ordinary person, else why would she have a name like that. Anyway, they never made her cry."

When the book begins, Wanda has already disappeared from school and no one thinks about her absence until she wins the girls' prize in the school-wide competition—for a hundred stunning illustrations of the dresses she had described to her classmates. Drawings that were once all lined up, in her closet.

It turns out that Wanda's family has moved to the big city where, her father writes in a letter to the teacher, life is much better: "No more holler Polack." Peggy and Maddie, who really do seem nice, want to find a way to make things up to Wanda, but they can't. In the end, Wanda is so forgiving that she asks the teacher to distribute her drawings among the girls, making sure that Peggy gets the green one, Maddie the blue, dresses modeled by girls that look like them. They realize that Wanda liked them in spite of the game.

My daughter was furious that *100 Dresses* deprived her of a more traditional catharsis—a group hug, perhaps, or an auditorium full of girls doing trust falls. "They never saw her again? I HATE THIS BOOK!" But I love the understated ending, which leaves Maddie—and us—with the image of the girl who never cried while other girls laughed at her.

Then again, in children's literature, the alphas rarely tell the story. Books are by betas, for betas, the wistful girls on the fringes of things.

I know this because I'm a beta who grew up to write books. I am a Maddie—in fact, my middle name is Madeline—currying favor with the brighter, prettier girls, who find temporary uses for my sharp tongue.

4.

Baltimore city schools students wear uniforms—khaki trousers, skirts, or jumpers paired with tops in their school's official color. I consider this to be one of the greatest things that has ever happened to me. No arguments with my daughter over what to wear, fewer clothes to buy. Most importantly, the uniform requirement helps to disguise class differences. Until you meet a kid's parents, it's impossible to figure out anyone's income or social standing.

My kid's school's catchment area is not particularly diverse in terms of race, an old Baltimore problem. But the class range is wide, as are the types of families. Two-parent, one-parent, no-parent. Two working parents, one working parent, no working parents. There are super-involved parents, which is part of the reason the school is a good one. There are parents and guardians who never attend a single school event.

I fall in the middle of the pack. If I didn't control my own work hours, I'd probably contribute even less than I do. No teacher has ever suspected my daughter's take-home projects of being my handiwork. Bake sale, sure, because I like to show off my baking skills. Chocolate bar sales, hard pass. ("Do you know who wins the chocolate bar contest?" I recently asked my daughter. "The kid whose parents exploit the most people.") My mantra, which my daughter can recite, is: *I do what I can do, so when I say I can't do something, you know that means I can't do it.*

The girl who tortured my daughter that day—when I finally got a good look at her, I couldn't be angry. Or maybe it was her mother who made my wrath dissipate. Glimpsing her at a school event, I was sure of one thing:

There was no way she had called the principal on me. This is a woman so exhausted that when asked to help her daughter with a school project, she—well, I can't tell you what happened, because that would identify them. Let's just say that it was a level of under-performance that would have been hilarious in a sitcom. In real life, it indicated a household dysfunction so profound that I decided her daughter's problems went well beyond meanness.

I also suspect her mom's not on Twitter and therefore did not see what I wrote that October afternoon:

There's a mean girl at my daughter's school and I want to kill her in a book. But her name won't work in a historical novel set in 1966 but I play a long game, kid.

5.

"Twitter," symbolized by the silhouette of a blue bird, is an onomatopoeia of birdsong, as is "tweet." Its very name suggests light, inconsequential chatter. However, there is no evidence that it has anything to do with Tweety Bird, the cartoon not-exactly-a-canary created by Bob Clampett.

Tweety, the bird of bulbous head and tiny body—"I

tawt I taw a puddy tat! I did! I did!"—was my hero when I was a kid. I vividly remember trick-or-treating as Tweety when I was three or four, in a cheap store-bought costume. Tweety always came out on top.

But Tweety, as it turns out, had a vicious streak when he started out. He wasn't just an innocent bystander, thwarting a determined predator. Tweety's origin story is a little tangled, but I've established this much: In his earliest outings, Tweety liked to bring the pain.

Maybe I do, too. Maybe that's why I always gravitated toward Tweety. Because while it's rare for me to start something, I will finish it. My ability for verbal cruelty is preternatural to the point that I have spent much of my life trying to curb it. As a teenager, I once said something so vicious that the affected person threw a glass of milk at my face. It whizzed by my ear and crashed to the floor.

Frankly, I deserved it.

What is a bully? What is bullying? The words are invoked so often that they have become meaningless. (Just watch a *Real Housewives* reunion and you'll see what I mean.) When everyone claims they are being bullied, does bullying even exist? Of course it does, but it's harder to define.

Am I a bully? Yeah, sometimes I think I am. Have I ever been a mean girl? I believe almost everyone tries on the persona at some point in her life. Because here's the dirty little secret—making fun of other people can be fun. Oh, I endeavor to do it the polite way, behind people's backs. I know that's not right, either, but it's hard to keep my X-Men-like power under wraps. I don't get to control the weather, I don't have retractable claws. But when I take my gloves off, I am lethal.

Here's one example: A former boss, someone who treated me terribly, was diagnosed with cancer. I shared the news with a friend who also had worked for him.

"Is it an aggressive cancer?" he asked, concerned despite his own intense dislike for the man.

"Oh, you know [him]," I said. "It's a passive-aggressive cancer."

Look, he's still alive, many years later. My words are cutting, but they're not all-powerful.

I had a much crueler comment about the girl who made my daughter unhappy. I won't repeat it here.

I will admit what I told my daughter to say when another classmate wondered why my daughter didn't wear a fancier dress for the awards presentation during the final week of school.

"Tell her this: I dressed casually because the third-grade award ceremony probably won't be the pinnacle of my life, but, hey, good move on your part wearing your best dress."

I tweeted that, too.

6.

As it turned out, the principal was not that mad at me. He had to contact me because of the Concerned Parents. What were the Concerned Parents so concerned about? I asked. Their fear was that I would use my access as a volunteer to confront the child. I laughed at the insanity of this idea. Many months later, I would learn that one of my friends had done just that, gotten into the face of a girl who had tortured her son and inquired how she would feel if she were called the same names.

But then—my friend is an alpha. And because I did not know this story when I met with the principal, I laughed heartily at the idea that I would use my access to the premises for some kind of vendetta. Writers are all talk.

Two days after I met with the principal about my mean tweet, my daughter came home from school and said she had had the best day ever. *What happened?* I asked, pleased for her. Three girls who never played with her had allowed her to play with them—because they were intrigued by the robotic pony she had brought to school for show-and-tell.

"They let you play with them because they wanted to play with your toy?"

"Yes!"

"And you had fun?"

"Yes, the most fun, although I had to be the baby when we played family and I don't like being the baby."

"But you had fun?"

"Yes!"

"You had fun because they were nice to you because you had something that they wanted?"

"Yes!"

I turned my head so my daughter would not see my eyes filling with tears. I hate unsolicited advice and being a parent means to be blanketed with it, assaulted by it, smothered with it, often by Concerned Parents. These Concerned Parents have so much to tell you about sleep and diet and routine and peanut butter and diapers and flu shots. Bicycle helmets and child safety seats. The Concerned Parents flood the zone, aka the school's Facebook page, with all their concerns. Does anyone have the third-grade spelling words? When is the awards assembly?

But no one, *no one*, ever tells you that perhaps the single worst thing about being a parent is the opportunity to relive every shitty moment of your own childhood, only it's more terrible now, because it's happening to the person you love most in the world, a person you would literally kill for, come to think about it, and there's not a damn thing you can do about it.

So I tweet. *I tawt I taw a mean girl.*

I did. I did.

My Life as a Villainess

had been creating villains on the page for about seven years when I finally became one. A newspaper reporter by day, I was a mystery novelist by—well, not by night, actually, but by earlier day, rising at six A.M. to write one thousand or so words about Tess Monaghan, a private investigator in my beloved Baltimore.

Tess met many bad people in my first seven novels—a brittle society matron, a murderous newspaper editor, a lecherous lobbyist, an obsessive collector, a serial killer. Despite what those thumbnail descriptions may suggest, I took my work seriously. My role model was no one less than Prometheus, who made humans in his own image, then stole fire from the gods to make up for the fact that he had no other gifts to bestow on his creations. (Prometheus had labored so lovingly over his creation that his brother, Epimetheus, took all the good stuff—speed, extraordinary sight and hearing—and gave them to the animals.) I strove to love all my creations, to breathe life into them, as Prometheus did. I told myself that I was willing to be chained to a rock and have my liver eaten daily, if that's what it took to make my characters vivid. Metaphorically.

Don't be fooled by the hifalutin classical allusions. Growing up, I spent far more time with the usual cartoon and cartoonish villains than I did with the classics. Snidely Whiplash, who kept tying Nell to the tracks, only—curses!—to be foiled again by Dudley Do-Right. Simon Bar Sinister, who battled Underdog for Sweet Polly Purebred, to whom I bear an uncanny resemblance. Batman's nemeses—the Joker, the Penguin, the Riddler, and the beguiling Catwoman, but in the camp context of the television show.

Yet the most vivid villain of my youth was, curiously, Daedalus, who appeared in a very ill-informed cartoon about Hercules. Perhaps you remember the theme song: *Hercules, people are safe when near him / Hercules, only the evil fear him!* Yet to my knowledge, Hercules and

Daedalus never met in classic mythology and would have no reason to be enemies if they did. Daedalus was far more tragic than evil, losing his son, Icarus, when they fled their Labyrinth-prison on wax wings.

Like most females drawn to bad guys, I was a lifelong good girl. I didn't understand people who cheated and lied or killed. I could construct novels about how these things might happen, but in the end I was as baffled by the venality of humans beings as private eye Tess Monaghan.

Then, in the space of eighteen months, I went through two painful breakups. First, I walked out on my marriage of seven years. A few months later, my employer at the time, *The Sun*, initiated divorce proceedings against me. Of course, the job action was not framed in those terms, but I was a veteran of marriage counseling by then. I knew what the beginnings of a breakup looked like. My employer was doing to me what I had done to my husband, putting me on notice by announcing, more or less out of the blue, a generic, indefinable dissatisfaction that did not respond to rational arguments. In both cases, someone had to change if the relationship was to go forward.

The difference was that the newspaper would have

reconciled with me if I mended my ways—stopped writing novels, admitted that I had no gods before it. I, on the other hand, was completely disingenuous with my husband. On the March weekend that I walked out the door with my laptop and suitcase, I was done, but I didn't put it that way in our subsequent telephone conversations or counseling sessions.

The seeds of my villainy began there, in one of those insufferably neutral-looking rooms where marriage counselors tend to work. I stared at the beige wall and the beige carpet while I lied and lied and lied. If he would do this, if he would do that, I said. But I knew there was nothing he could do. I wanted out.

It's easier to talk about the job than about the husband. I was the wronged party in my job. My only fault there was finding a modest success outside the newspaper. And, as I've admitted, being far less deferential than the top boss required.

But, like the Michelle Pfeiffer version of Catwoman, I quickly morphed from victim to antagonist, filing a grievance against the company for the job actions taken against me. I did, in fact, the very things that my estranged husband could not bring himself to do in our divorce. I fought back. I used every legal tool available to me. Even before I fell into disfavor, I knew the union contract pretty well and understood my rights as an employee. Few reporters exercised those clauses and whereases and subparts. The bosses liked to think that fair treatment was a privilege they bestowed and they resented any suggestion that I had a say in such matters. But they were already angry with me. I had nothing to lose.

However, the tantrums and rage required by my new outlaw status did not come naturally to me, and a physical toll was exacted. I cracked two back molars from incessant grinding, creating a chain reaction of dental problems—crowns, an infection beneath the crowns, root canal, surgery when the root canal failed. I had stomachaches, headaches, insomnia, and a general sense of anxiety that was wholly new to me. In New Orleans for my first Mardi Gras, I bought a blank journal and resolved in its pages to give up fear for Lent. I didn't succeed. The two breakups ground on, bogged down in legalities and processes.

A year passed and my work arbitration had been delayed for several months. I became convinced that the bosses were trying to drive me crazy. The psychiatrist who had guided me through my decision to end my marriage wrote an open-ended medical excuse, saying I was not to return to work until the grievance was resolved.

The company responded by sending me to its chosen shrink. During my consultation, I learned a great deal about him, perhaps more than he learned about me. He had been a Navy SEAL. He had a World Series ring because he had worked with the Orioles during the team's 1983 championship season. He was, he told me, so brilliant and accomplished that many of his colleagues envied him. I think he was trying to create a bond between us, but I wanted no part of it.

"I don't see myself that way, and I don't act that way," I said. "I just want to be treated like any other employee, judged by the work I do while I'm on the clock, and not penalized for what I do when I'm not there."

"But you're *not* like the other employees," he told me cheerfully. "You have to get used to that."

In the end, the company's hired gun agreed with my doctor: I should not return to work until this matter was settled. A hearing was scheduled, but I was offered a confidential settlement in which neither side admitted fault.

The same week that my employer and I came to terms, I finalized the paperwork for the financial dissolution of my marriage. It was a brilliant autumn day and I was wandering around the streets of Baltimore, going to banks and brokerages, transferring funds, trying to find a notary to press his seal into the agreement my husband and I had finally reached. I waited twenty minutes to see the notary in one bank, only to be told that I needed an account there to use the notary's services. I burst into tears. I burst into tears a lot back then. I had burst into tears the moment I met the psychologist who evaluated me at my employer's request.

I had been ruthless about protecting my financial interests in my divorce. I was the sole breadwinner in our household, a setup to which I had agreed after we had been married two years. True, one could argue that I had been coerced, manipulated, even bullied into that arrangement, but the fact remains—I signed up for it and, initially, I liked it. No, we didn't have children and he didn't do quite as much cooking and cleaning as I thought a stay-at-home spouse should, but I knew how family law would treat us if it were truly gender-blind. Maryland is a marital property state, in which spouses are entitled to a fifty-fifty split of everything acquired during the marriage. This meant I had to give up half of my retirement accounts, half of the equity in the house I had owned before we married. The trickier part was determining what I owed my husband from my novel-writing. He proposed I simply give him fifty cents on the dollar on every dollar I made for the rest of my life.

"That's not happening," I emailed him. And I went to war. A quiet, sneaky war, but a war nonetheless.

Just two months before the frenzy of paperwork that led me to the bank, I had been offered a new three-book contract that would allow me to quit my day job. But the contract was still being negotiated, which meant it did not apply to my divorce settlement. Or so my lawyer advised me.

I also counted on my husband's passivity to keep him from finding legal representation on his own. True to his temperament, he had visited a few lawyers, but asked them to work on contingency, something divorce attorneys are not wont to do, especially when the stakes are so small. My own lawyer, who had represented Tom Clancy's first wife, did everything she could to keep my bills small. "The two cases have a lot or similarities in terms of intellectual property," she told me. "But the money is *quite* different."

Recently, I had reason to go into my divorce file and I discovered an email I wrote my lawyer during the back-and-forth over the financial settlement. We had sent my husband a proposal, only to have him rewrite it completely, line by line. The puzzling part was that he didn't want more money. If anything, he was shortchanging himself. He just wanted to dictate the terms. "It's important to him to feel he's in charge," I explained to my lawyer in an email, "even if it means ending up with less." By then I had spent seven years explaining him to the outside world. It was second nature to me. I knew him as well as I've ever known anyone, and when the time came, I exploited that knowledge ruthlessly.

In the end, he got 50 percent of my retirement funds, a fairly new Ford Explorer, and enough cash to live comfortably, without working at all, for at least two years.

And he got 100 percent of himself. The price I had to pay for leaving him was him. That wasn't written down anywhere, but it was always understood. I would never again speak to the one person who had encouraged me to follow my dreams, to write that first book. The one person who was there at the beginning, who knows how long the road was, is never there when good news arrives in the form of a royalty check or a film sale.

So I found myself twice divorced, from my husband and my job. I had no regrets. But when I sat down to start my eighth novel, I knew something new about venality—my own. I realized that somewhere in Texas, where my ex had settled, a person woke up every day and cursed me as a villain. Well, probably not cursed and probably not every day. That's a little self-aggrandizing. But, to the extent that he did think of me, it was in the shape of a most unflattering narrative. *I loved her, I believed in her and then, just as she was on the verge of becoming successful, she left me.* I had become the bad guy in someone else's story.

And I deserved it.

My friends and family argue with me about this. I find it helps if I flip the genders in my story. Imagine a husband, encouraged by a loving wife who believes in him utterly and lets him roll the dice for the big score. Then, just as the gamble is about to pay off, husband sheds wife.

We know what we say about such men. They're bounders, jerks, solipsists. One of the great ironies of my life is that I achieved gender parity by becoming an asshole.

It turns out the *Mighty Hercules* cartoon wasn't so far off the mark, after all. Daedalus was a killer, the worst sort. It's easy to forget there was a reason he had been sent to Crete. Daedalus threw his nephew Talus off the Acropolis in a fit of envy. At Minos's direction, Daedalus built the Labyrinth to contain the Minotaur. He then told Theseus how to slay that poor monster-child, which is why Minos imprisoned Daedalus and Icarus in the Labyrinth. Other than Theseus, no one behaves nobly in this particular myth. Minos is, essentially, the Minotaur's stepfather, and he is ashamed of the child, the result of his wife's coupling with a bull. True, the Minotaur eats any human he meets, but can you blame him, would you use his limitations to destroy him? Rereading the myth, I feel a pang for that poor creature, a prisoner of his mutant nature.

Still, if you encounter him in his lair, it's him or you. Which one would you choose?

As a newly minted villain, I have more empathy for my invented ones. I find I can live inside the skull of just about anyone—a pair of eleven-year-old killers, a man who menaces his girlfriend's children, a high school girl with a gun, a teenage drug dealer, a woman who will do anything to protect her child. I have learned that few people, outside of real sociopaths, wake up in the morning, look in the mirror, laugh a villainous laugh, and twirl a mustache, imaginary or no, proclaiming: "I am EEEEE-VIL." No, most of us just blunder and rationalize our way into doing the unthinkable, step by sneaky step. I was unhappy. I wanted to be happy, and that required making someone else miserable.

I wouldn't hesitate to do it again.

Part IV
Genius

*How many geniuses does it
take to change a light bulb?
Only one. Thomas Edison.*

[From a Reddit forum]

A Fine Bromance

1.

Leonard Cohen died the night before the 2016 U.S. presidential election, but the news was not yet public when I got up and put on my black pantsuit to go vote. It would be three days before a record company confirmed the singer-songwriter's passing. By then I was with American friends in Italy, tender and jet-lagged, feeling like someone who had watched through the rearview window of the last spaceship out as my beloved home planet exploded. When we heard about Cohen, a friend began streaming his best-known song, "Hallelujah," on her phone. And I felt—nothing.

This wasn't new for me. It had been more than a decade since I could muster actual grief about a famous person's death. "I don't *know* him," I explained to my shocked friends.

Since that night in Italy, these friends check in when a celebrity dies, curious to see if the event has moved the needle on my cold, stony heart. Prince, Peggy Lipton, Doris Day, Luke Perry, Burt Reynolds, Frank Robinson, Philip Roth, Albert Finney, Dr. John, Barbara Bush, Peter Tork—the list goes on and on. Unfortunately, inevitably. I was indifferent more often than not. Even when I experienced a flicker of emotion—Robinson, Roth, Tork, Dr. John—it wasn't about the deceased. It was about me, where they resided in my memories. Watching the Monkees as a dorky eight-year-old, filling a shelf with Roth's complete works as a dorky twenty-five-year-old, trying to decipher whatever the fuck Dr. John says in *The Last Waltz*, and, years later, riding an elevator in the Hotel Monteleone with him as a dorky fifty-year-old.

I shyly confided I was a fan. "You just keep on doing what you do, darlin'," said the Doctor.

My lack of emotion when famous people die is probably a character flaw. I won't challenge the legitimacy of your grief in the wake of a celebrity's death, I promise. I'm okay if you want to build a spontaneous shrine, toss another teddy bear on the pile. But I am skeptical of those social media sob sisters who appear to be gutted by every celebrity passing.

In part, my reaction, or lack thereof, is a by-product of twenty years as a journalist; famous dead people generated work, the kind of work I liked least, in which reporters were dispatched to ask random people how they *felt*. Princess Diana, John F. Kennedy Jr.—I remember staring at the editor who assigned me to write about those two tragic deaths, wondering what in hell I had to add to the discourse. I know W. H. Auden had bigger fish to fry in "September 1, 1939," when he criticized "the folded lie, the romantic lie in the brain of the sensual man in the street." But whenever I come across those lines, it feels to me as if Auden once pounded the pavement as a reporter, dutifully asking randos their reactions to news stories.

I'm a tough old bird, in case that's not clear by now.

You don't want to know what I do with my daughter's artwork.

June 8, 2018, was different. I dropped my kid at school, then walked to a neighborhood coffee shop to work on a novel due by month's end. A silly thought popped into my head and I resolved to tweet it before I began my morning writing session. I opened my laptop and my plans immediately changed: My Twitter timeline was filling with news that Anthony Bourdain had been found dead, an apparent suicide. In my memory, it's like a cinematic montage, or one of those close-ups on a computer screen in which a message emerges keystroke by keystroke, faster and faster. *Bourdain found dead. Bourdain is dead, a suicide. Bourdain, dead. #RIPBourdain.*

I burst into tears. Bourdain wasn't my friend, more of a friend-in-law via my spouse, who had wooed him in a sense, won him, ended up working with him. But I had been the Cyrano in their love story, telling my husband the right words to say.

Was I crying for Bourdain, or was I crying for my husband? Was I crying because the circumstances—suicide, a young daughter left behind—were unfathomable to me? Or was I crying for myself? If so, wasn't that unseemly, a variation of the performative Internet mourning that I so loathe?

Almost two years later, I'm still trying to answer these questions.

2.

When my daughter was younger, every child she met was automatically her friend. "Where's my friend?" she would ask minutes after saying goodbye to a strange kid who had played with her at the playground.

But she could never remember anyone's name. Everyone was just "friend." Specifically, *my* friend. "Where's my friend?" "Are we going to see my friend?" "What happened to my friend?"

Eventually, I suggested that one way to make really good friends was to learn people's names. She took my advice to heart. Her two besties are A—and D—. These are stormy, passionate relationships, up and down, more twists than a soap opera. I recently found this note on the dining room table:

Dear G—

thank you for being my friend! I hope you have good holidays and birthdays for the rest of your life! I hope we will be friends forever!

Love, D—

People can be disdainful of the exclamation mark, but I think we should use it more, at least when corresponding with our friends.

3.

"I want to be his friend," my husband told me, pointing at the television screen. It was Labor Day weekend 2009 and he had spent much of it on the sofa with his teenage son, watching Anthony Bourdain in a *No Reservations* marathon. "I feel that we could be good friends if we met."

I reminded him that we had, in fact, met Bourdain nine years earlier, albeit glancingly, an exchange Bourdain could not be expected to remember. But they shared a mutual acquaintance, a magazine editor. Surely he could connect them.

A few days later, I came home to find my husband pacing. The editor had given him a phone number. A phone number! He had hoped for an email address, which would allow him to impress and flatter with his erudite style. *What was he going to do with a phone number?*

I coached him the way a doting mother might instruct her son how to call a girl for the first time.

"You're working on a project set in New Orleans, with a chef character," I said. "Call Bourdain and tell him you want to take him to lunch to pick his brain about chef patois, the kind of details only real kitchen workers would know. One condition—if this scheme succeeds, you have to take me with you."

Three months later, we met at Sushi Yasuda in New York City. By that point, I was so committed to our bit that I was carrying a notebook, in which I occasionally jotted down Bourdain's insights about kitchen life. Did we remind him of our earlier meeting? Probably, but only because that story has a good punch line.

It was at a crime writers conference in Manchester,

England, in October 2000. *Kitchen Confidential* had been published earlier that year and it was already clear that it would overshadow Bourdain's promising start as a crime novelist. There was a palpable sense of people pulling at him, wanting his attention, his approval. David and I introduced ourselves and he immediately apologized for his unkind words about our hometown in *Kitchen Confidential*.

"I was still using then," he said, "and I couldn't score. It made me irritable."

"You couldn't find heroin in Baltimore?" I replied. "You are the most incompetent addict that ever lived."

Or did I? I think I did. Maybe I started the joke and David finished it. No, I'm pretty sure it was my joke. My husband is a brilliant man, one of the most articulate people I know. I am still amazed, after almost two decades with him, by the beautifully formed sentences and ideas that flow from him, his ability to speak in complete sentences, paragraphs, pages. But—you'll have to take my word for this—I'm the funny one. I may be the beta to his alpha, but I'm the funny one.

At our lunch, I did a thing that I think most betas do—I

covertly studied Bourdain, the alpha in this situation, and made sure to follow his protocol. He eschewed soy sauce, so I did, too.

My husband was so flustered that he not only drowned his sashimi in soy sauce, he ended up pouring soy sauce into his sake cup.

4.

It is the early months of 2019 and I am working on an essay about how much I love my double boiler. The first draft includes a paragraph about my weakness for those kitchen essential lists compiled by food writers and chefs I admire, including Bourdain. I credit Bourdain with my use of squeeze bottles, clarifying that I took that tip from his book before I met him.

The editor suggests I take out the fact that I knew Bourdain personally. "Sounds kind of braggy," he writes on my copy.

Over the course of edits, the entire paragraph is jettisoned as the piece goes in a different direction, but I can't stop thinking about that note, *Sounds kind of braggy.*

Would he have written this on my husband's copy? I
think not. Was I bragging?

Probably.

5.

The same autumn in 2000 that we introduced ourselves
to Bourdain for the first time, the real first time, David
and I met one of my literary heroes, James Crumley, at
yet another crime writers conference.

The event, programmed by not-yet-juggernaut Har-
lan Coben, was a mix of old and new. The elder states-
men were people like Crumley, Donald Westlake, Evan
Hunter, and Paco Ignacio Taibo II. The "young" folks—in
their thirties and forties—included Coben, Dennis Lehane, George Pelecanos, and me.

But while Westlake and Hunter were a little aloof—
not unfriendly, just not up for long evenings in the bar—
Crumley loved being with younger writers who hung on
his every word. He told stories on himself, graciously in-
habiting his legend. The only one I remember involved
trying to snort cocaine off a knife blade while driving a
car down a Texas highway, then hitting a bump in the

road and slicing open his nostril right before he sailed into a speed trap.

Years later, a writer-friend who had known Crumley much longer than I, going back to the 1980s, gently reminded me that Jim's larger-than-life reputation came at a cost for some, especially his four ex-wives and his children.

But Jim had mellowed by the time I met him. He was happy in his fifth marriage, grateful to be lionized. Our paths crossed only three times in eight years, but we emailed a little and I interviewed him once for a fanzine. It was a phone conversation, quiet and unrushed, the kind of exchange we could never have at a crime writers conference. When I saw him in public settings, there was always someone trying to jostle me out of the way. Usually I let them. I was confident enough in Jim's affection and admiration to let the fanboys have their moment.

Still, I had projected a lot onto Jim, an inevitable by-product of hero worship. In our interview, which turned out to be our last conversation, he disabused me of several of those notions. (He was literally feeling no pain—he had just come from dental surgery and was drinking French vodka through a straw.) I had assumed, for example, that a former roughneck from South Texas would have found the University of Iowa Writers' Workshop pretentious and twee, but Jim told me fervently it was like heaven. Montana, his residence of choice, was another kind of heaven. He had yearned to be a poet, but accepted an early mentor's verdict that his talent was for prose. He confirmed for me a long-rumored story that he had once thrown one of his manuscripts into a fire pit, destroying the only copy. He mourned the loss of a favorite book, one of the twelve volumes in Anthony Powell's *Dance to the Music of Time*, taken by a girl from Trinidad, Colorado.

Less than two years later, Jim was dead at the age of sixty-eight.

I was in Glasgow, Scotland, a hanger-on for my husband's book tour. It was September, the days were already short and cool. I put on my coat and stalked through the early dusk, grateful to be in a different time zone than the U.S., where Facebook and the comments sections on popular blogs were filling with reminiscences from people who didn't know Jim. And maybe I didn't know him that well, either. (I'm not sure you can call someone a friend unless they have a set of your spare house keys.) But I knew him better than most of his public mourners did.

There was one poseur in particular, a bad writer and a worse person, who had wrung quite a few words out of once being in the same bar with Jim. He claimed that Jim had caught his eye and they had exchanged knowing glances, potential kindred spirits. *I imagined him thinking that we would be friends*, he wrote, or words to that effect.

Oh my god, I thought, *Jim would have HATED you.*

Except he wouldn't have. Jim was an inclusive, gregarious fellow. He didn't judge people by their backlists or their reviews. If you came to the table and told a good story, he would welcome your company.

I never got over the posturing that I saw in the wake of Jim's death. By the time one is sixty, there have been a lot of memorial services. Again and again, I am shocked by how often the tributes are really about the speaker. Not always, maybe not even most of the time. But there's always at least one eugoogoolizer, to use Derek Zoolander's inimitable term, who ends up telling everyone how much the deceased loved and admired the living person.

6.

"Am I famous?" my daughter asks me frequently. "Am I a little bit famous? Am I famous for a kid?"

"We tweet about you, sometimes, your dad and I. But we don't use your real name or show your face. So, yeah, people who have never met you know about you."

"Are *you* famous?" she asks me.

"No. Maybe Baltimore-famous."

"What's Baltimore-famous?"

"It means that I can never be rude in public because there's a slight chance I will be recognized. And no one should be rude in public anyway."

"Is Daddy famous?"

"Yes, Daddy's kind of famous. You don't remember this, but when you were only three years old, a man recognized him on a corner in Barcelona. And one time, he went to a Dublin pub for a pint and the newspaper was tipped off and they sent someone to take his photograph."

"Can Daddy make me famous? Will he put me in his show?"

"Um—maybe one day."

Daddy's show at the time was about porn.

7.

Bourdain was the most famous person I knew. Not *met*—I was a reporter, after all, I was once bear-hugged by Boris Yeltsin, who thought I was part of his welcoming party when I was doing the journalistic duty known as "death watch," in which your job is to report back to the desk that the famous person visiting your city is still alive. I interviewed presidents and would-be presidents; the only shouting match of my newspaper career was with George W. Bush, then campaigning for his father.

My husband's work has allowed me to mingle with famous people in the entertainment industry. My job as a novelist has led to my acquaintanceships with celebrities. I exchange holiday cards with a couple of really famous actresses, but I'm not going to share their names. Too braggy.

But Bourdain was an international celebrity, his reach amplified by CNN when he moved to that channel for what would be his last television show, *Parts Unknown*. There's a description of James Bond, often attributed to Raymond Chandler, but more likely the work of *London Times* reviewer Raymond Mortimer—men want to be him, women want to be with him. (Mortimer actually wrote: "Men want to be him, women want him between the sheets.") For Bourdain, I would alter it slightly: Men wanted to be him or be his friend—and women did, too.

Knowing Bourdain, even as a friend-in-law, had many perks. First and foremost was his company; I socialized with him only twice, but it was a joy. He was very much the person one saw on TV—funny, profane, incredibly smart.

He invited our household to a boucherie in Louisiana, a tail-to-snout pig-eating festival in which Bourdain assassinated the pig on camera. (I passed because I didn't think our toddler daughter could handle the summer heat.) He arranged for David and me to skip the line at an incomparable Paris bistro; of course, the reason the line was so long was because Bourdain had featured it on one of his television shows. He recruited famous chefs to play themselves on my husband's post-Katrina Valentine to New Orleans, *Treme*, where Bourdain had, in fact, ended up working in the writers' room. As a result, I met several chefs I admire, including Tom Colicchio, David Chang, Wylie Dufresne, and Eric Ripert.

Somehow, Ripert decided he owed David a favor and encouraged him to dine at his restaurant, Le Bernardin. The night we were there, Henry Kissinger was at a nearby table. My husband became agitated. On the one hand, he was Ripert's guest. On the other hand, he was sitting a few feet away from a war criminal. He wanted to throw a drink on him, or worse. But he contained his impulses out of respect for Ripert.

At the meal's end, we were served a dessert that I don't believe can be ordered, a scooped-out egg filled with creamy, sweet layers. Ripert, in a visit to our table, told us that the egg was reserved for special friends of the restaurant.

"DOES KISSINGER GET AN EGG?" my husband asked. David and Bourdain shared many things, but a virulent hatred of Kissinger was definitely at the top of the list. Off and on, over the years, they had talked about a project based on the book *Legacy of Ashes*, a history of the CIA. It was, in fact, one of the last things they ever spoke about, in the fall of 2017.

Ripert was the person who found Bourdain's body on June 8, 2018. It has become my practice to write notes to people who have lost close friends to death; it seems to me they are often overlooked when someone passes. But the note I wrote to Ripert is still in my desk, addressed and stamped, never sent. I felt I had no standing to offer him my condolences.

I even felt weird about being the person who broke the news to my husband, who was temporarily banned from Twitter on the day that Bourdain died.

I was surprised to learn, in a tribute that David wrote the same day, that I had made David feel bad by pointing out that Bourdain did not put soy sauce on his sushi, much less in his sake cup. He wrote on his blog: *Later, walking back across town, I replayed that submoronic moment to my wife, who laughed and made it so much worse by noting that Bourdain himself had savored Naomichi Yasuda's fare without soy sauce at all.*

That was not my intent. I'm pretty sure that was not my intent. I was laughing at myself, my tendency to study others and follow their leads. My husband doesn't have to do that. I do.

I recently mentioned to David that I was trying to

write about Bourdain and celebrity death culture and who gets to be whose friend and who is entitled to mourn whom. "Of course, I wasn't his friend," I added quickly. "That's sort of what I'm working out, how and why one gets to mourn the death of someone they don't really know. But you were his friend."

"I really was," he said, his voice full of wonder. He had pointed to a television, yearning for connection to the person he saw, but then he made the connection. Thousands of people felt the same way, but David made it happen. He told the story, again, of the last night they saw each other, the email Bourdain sent the next morning, about *Legacy of Ashes*. It was as sweet and true and sincere as "D—'s" note to my daughter, albeit with fewer exclamation marks and more expletives. They had hoped to be friends forever.

I just wish they had gotten the chance to bum-rush Henry Kissinger together, although not in Le Bernadin.

8.

When I taught creative writing to college-age students, I could always count on one or two suicide stories per semester. I could also rely on those stories to portray suicide as beautiful, noble, inspiring, etc. My favorite, by far, will sound silly in the telling, but I have come to love it unironically: A beautiful young woman, wealthy in all material ways, takes to her bath, determined to slit her wrists with her grandfather's straight razor. The family retainer—a gardener–butler–jack-of-all-trades—is so well trained in caring for the family that he intuits the young woman's desire and tries to help her out by shooting her. She becomes furious at the idea that any man would try to take agency over her life. She flings the straight razor at him, slitting his throat or piercing his heart, I forget. The story ends with her stepping out of the bath and over the body of the dead gardener.

But I guess that's not really a suicide story, is it? I love it because the girl decides to live. The eternal problem with suicide stories is that the people who have the answers are never here to provide them.

9.

In October 2019, there was an Internet auction of Bourdain's possessions. I was flush, having signed a new contract. I studied the online catalog of 202 items, aware that I could buy something if I so desired. But *should* I? If I did, what would I choose? The collection of 45s would be a perfect gift for my husband. The Michelin Bibendum statue could mingle almost seamlessly with my collection of robots made from found kitchen objects. Bourdain's desk might be the cornerstone of an elaborate office makeover I was secretly planning for myself.

Within just a few days, the auction items attracted bids at multiples of their value. The more personal the item, the more extreme the gap between its estimated value and the bid. Item #87, a chef's knife with a certificate of authenticity, had an estimated value of $4,000–$6,000. It had been bid up to $21,000 by the auction's fourth day.

Meanwhile, the Bibendum, with an estimated value of $150–$250, zoomed to more than $5,000, then soared past $10,000. I sincerely yearned for it, except—how could I yearn for an object I hadn't even known existed before the auction? True, it looked like the type of thing I collect and I had delicious memories of a dinner at a place called Bibendum during my honeymoon with David. But the Bourdain Bibendum, a gift to him from Chef Marco Pierre—it had no connection to the memory I wanted to celebrate. If a Bibendum was all I wanted, the Internet was full of them, for much less than $10,000.

I was vexed. How could I justify buying something at several times its actual value just because it had belonged to a famous person who was my husband's friend? Who was bidding on these items? What were they seeking? Bourdain was always self-deprecating about his chef skills and the knife was a fairly recent acquisition. Given that he told the *New Yorker* he was home only twenty weeks out of the year, how many times had he wielded it, what had he prepared using it? If one didn't have a profound personal connection with Bourdain, what was the point of owning his knife? Can you imagine winning an item at auction—a pair of sunglasses or the Zippo lighter, say—then feeling the urge to tell people that it had been touched by the hand of Bourdain? What was the point? Yet the proceeds would go to his daughter and estranged wife, who had committed to donating 40 percent of the total to a scholarship in his name at the Culinary Institute of America. What was the harm?

My head hurt. The only person who could have made sense out of the Bourdain auction was Bourdain himself.

The auction ended October 30, item by item, with

two-minute gaps between each one. By 9:08 A.M., Eastern time, the Bibendum had sold for more than $61,000, 245 times its estimated valued. An hour or so later, item #87, the knife, fetched the highest price as expected, a total of $231,250 when the "buyer's premium" of 25 percent was added to the $185,000 bid. In total, almost $2 million was raised.

During the month that the auction was live, I would visit the website almost daily and study the items, wondering if I dared to bid. Finally, I decided I would allow myself to submit exactly one bid for one thing and never increase it. If I won, I would give the object to David, Bourdain's true friend, for Hanukkah 2019.

I would love to tell you what the item was, how much I bid, if I won, but—naw, too braggy.

Saving Mrs. Banks

1.

The year my daughter was born, every crib and stroller in America was recalled.

Hyperbole, but not by much. In July 2010, when my six-week-old daughter was still sleeping in a basket by our bedside, the U.S. Consumer Protection Agency announced that the manufacture of drop-sided cribs must end within the year. The cribs were blamed for at least 30 and maybe as many as 150 deaths; when you dig into the research, it's difficult to pinpoint precise numbers. The statistics on the crib recalls are firmer: 3 million in 2010, 11 million over a three-year period. Hand-me-down cribs were considered especially dangerous. We had just such a crib in our storage unit, where it had waited almost sixteen years to serve another Simon scion. Toodle-loo, toots.

Two million Graco strollers also were recalled in 2010 because four children had been fatally strangled in them. This followed a recall of the Maclaren stroller, *the* choice of upwardly mobile families, an alert issued after reports that a faulty mechanism had amputated at least a dozen children's fingers.

Meanwhile, the car seat we had chosen at—oh, sweet Jesus, what a name—buybuy Baby was so repugnant to the woman whose job was to help new parents with car seat installation that she refused to visit us if we didn't replace it. We didn't.

Somehow, our daughter survived it all. She survived the Bumbo seat, a piece of molded plastic designed to help babies sit up. It, too, was recalled and retrofitted with a safety belt, although if one looks closely at the Bumbo accidents, they appear to be the result of parents putting the Bumbo on elevated surfaces *despite being warned not to put the Bumbo on elevated surfaces.*

Not that I would ever criticize any parent for this kind of mistake: During a two A.M. feeding when my daughter was not even a week old, I came perilously close to dropping her on her head when I started dozing off while watching a DVRed episode of *Glee*. And, yes, I knew the books said that one shouldn't do feedings in front of the television. But it was the first season, when *Glee* was still good.

Besides, I had given up pretty quickly on the what-to-expect books when I was expecting. The guides to pregnancy were irrelevant to my maternity journey, while the books on a child's first year struck me as fearmongering polemics that kept circling back to breastfeeding. *You can do it. You really should do it. You better do it.*

These admonitions seemed silly to me. How does a fifty-one-year-old never-pregnant woman breastfeed a child? *You can do it if you're motivated*, one book insisted. No, it really did. If I wanted to coax breast milk from my perimenopausal, never-pregnant body, I just needed to give it the old college try.

So no books for me. I picked up information as I always had, from context and my own mistakes. I sort-of childproofed—covering up outlets, installing baby gates, eliminating obvious dangers. My sister and I have almost identical scars beneath our eyebrows, the legacy of a sharp-cornered coffee table in our parents' living room, so I knew to look for dangerous edges at knee-height, but I also knew such cuts weren't fatal. To this day, I'm not sure I ever installed the car seat correctly. And it's a toss-up whether my pro-germ stance was a philosophy or a rationalization, but it seems to have worked well for us. My kid is hardy. She has to be.

I remember lying awake the first night she slept in the new crib I had assembled, straining my ears to hear the tiniest turn of a screw. The crib was fine. Me, not so much.

Bad cribs, bad car seats, bad strollers, bad Mom. These were the first three months of my daughter's life.

In month four, we found Yaya.

Mary Poppins came in when the wind blew from the east. Our nanny arrived from sixteen hundred miles to the southwest because, five years earlier, Hurricane Katrina had blown through New Orleans and the levees had given way, disrupting her education at Tulane. It truly is an ill wind, et cetera, et cetera, et cetera.

2.

The first challenge in hiring a nanny was confronting the very word "nanny." My husband and I are solidly middle-class people no matter what our tax return says. We grew up in comfortable households with weekly cleaning ladies; childcare wasn't an issue because our mothers didn't work outside the home until we were old enough to be on our own. We do have some indulgences—our vacations skew fancy, we love good food, I wouldn't tell anyone what I pay for my hair color and cut—but we pretty much live as we did when we met as newspaper colleagues thirty years ago. In creating a job description for our childcare provider, our only model was the Washington Baltimore Newspaper Guild contract.

To repeat—not nanny people.

A nanny is Mary Poppins or Ole Golly, the wise woman who took care of Harriet the Spy. A nanny is someone who lives under your roof, which held zero appeal for me. Live-in help? No, never, no way. The problem was that we would be bouncing between Baltimore, our home, and New Orleans, where my husband needed to work six months out of the year for an unknown amount of time.

This meant we needed someone who was cool moving back and forth between two cities. Yet we couldn't offer housing in New Orleans, only in Baltimore—the bedroom above my office, in a separate rowhouse. Okay, our other indulgence is real estate. We had bought a nearby, falling-apart rowhouse in 2007—note the uncanny timing, right before the global economic collapse—thinking my parents could live there one day. "I'd never live in your neighborhood," my father said, "it's dirty and there's no parking." He was right on all counts: It's dirty, there's no parking, and he died in 2014 in his own bed. My father, an editorial writer, would do almost anything to win an argument.

Imagine my husband and me as Jane and Michael Banks in the movie version of *Mary Poppins*, singing this list to childcare agencies.

> If you want this sweet child care gig,
> Know your job won't be all that big.
> Eight hours per day
> Too much? Okay.
> You must travel between two cities.
> If you get airsick that's a pity
> Understand Mom is super-dumb
> Dad means well but is on the run.
> Always be calm, composed.

Keep your expectations low.
Pardon us if this sounds sappy
We just want you to be happy.
The only model for your employment:
A union contract, so max enjoyment.
We won't drink then overshare
And make you squirm,
Saddle you with housework
Or eat the mezcal worm.
(*David, proudly: That's the part I put in*)

Hurry, Nanny!
Many thanks.
Sincerely,
David and Laura Not-Banks

Much as the Banks children's letter had to reconstitute itself and fly on the breeze to find its way to Mary Poppins, our words were cast wide. Advised by a usually sensible friend who swore the universe would send what I needed, I tried everything, told everyone. I contacted the LISTSERV used by families in our neighborhood. No one had any suggestions, but local gossips had great fun spreading the word that the dude behind *The Wire* needed a nanny. I added discretion to the list of our future nanny's requirements.

We were running out of time when my husband's assistant came up with a candidate. One of her high school friends had moved to New Orleans to attend college but was now working as a full-time babysitter and in search of a new gig. Given that her parents lived forty-five minutes from our South Baltimore home, she liked the idea of a job that came with free trips back to Maryland at least once a month.

I'm not going to lie, I was tempted not to check her references. I called exactly one.

In a scary movie, this would have been my downfall. Nannies come in only two flavors in our culture, perfect and deadly. But this was not a scary movie, and besides, as already established, the world itself was a fraught hellscape in which everyday essentials were trying to kill my child, with the occasional assist from me. I had nothing to lose, except more time away from work.

Enter Yaya.

3.

Our household keeps fairly detailed Google calendars, but there is no mention of the moment that Sara K. met GR, the family shorthand for our child's name. I am certain that she started the job before October 1, 2010, her twenty-fourth birthday, as September 27, 2010, bears a notation that would be repeated many times over the next four years: *LL/GRS/SK travel.* We were on planes twice a month; my daughter achieved frequent flyer status on Southwest Airlines every year until she started school at the age of four.

Sara is a beautiful woman with long brown hair and green eyes. (If this line appeared in a manuscript in one of my fiction-writing workshops, I would annotate it and query my student: "DO YOU KNOW HOW RARE GREEN EYES ARE IN THE GENERAL POPULA-TION? Also, 'beautiful' is kind of generic.") She has an infectious laugh and a natural ease that cannot be faked. I know, I've tried. Her nickname, Yaya, came from GR's first attempts to say "Sara." People are often surprised upon meeting her because they assumed "Yaya" to be an elderly Greek grandmother.

Yaya is not only not elderly, she is very much a woman of her adopted hometown, New Orleans, known as the city that care forgot. On the clock, she was the most responsible person I have ever met. Off, she was still responsible, but focused on fun. It's hard not to have fun in New Orleans, but Sara is especially good at a particular kind of low-key revelry, the constant churn of crawfish boils, Mardi Gras masquerade balls, music festivals.

She became a full-time babysitter shortly after Katrina threw a monkey wrench into her education at Tulane. She was, in a word, a word I had never really been able to define before I met Sara, unflappable. She also fit in seamlessly wherever we traveled, and we traveled a lot. Everyone adored Sara. The other teachers at the Florida workshop where I taught every January, my dearest friend in London, my family, my writer friends, the Baltimore neighborhood moms. She made every room a little sunnier, every experience a little breezier. Or, as she taught GR to say: Easy-peasy, lemon squeezy.

Over the four years she worked for us, Sara would:

Tell me when to start feeding my daughter solid food.

Show me how to make toddler-appropriate solid food.

Teach my daughter sign language so she could communicate her needs while preverbal.

Toilet-train my daughter.

Show me various homeopathic remedies for teething.

Take full responsibility for the diaper bag, to the extent that I am still struggling, five years later, to remember to travel with snacks and Kleenex.

Face down TSA in Newark International Airport when an agent challenged her right to travel alone with a one-year-old child who was not her own. They missed the plane, but Sara won the battle. I abandoned a business trip to rescue them.

Patch a tire on a rental car in Italy while alone with a three-year-old on a country road, drive it gently into town, then call a friend of mine to come get her because she didn't want to interrupt my day visit to Siena.

Make it through a New Orleans–to–Baltimore flight with an uncharacteristically hysterical GR and a broken ankle, about which she never complained. (To be fair, she didn't know it was broken, thought it was a bad sprain, and I gave her time off for surgery and recuperation. Yay me!)

Over those four years I would:

Write four novels.

Write Sara a check every week.

Take Sara to Florida, the Pacific Northwest, New York, London, Spain, Australia, New Zealand, and Italy.

Climb the Sydney Bridge with Sara.

Ask Sara to accompany us to what was then the #1 restaurant in the world where we had scored a reservation unexpectedly. To this day, I keep a photo in my phone of Sara next to my stepson, Ethan, giving an enthusiastic thumbs-up as we sat down to a twenty-course, four-hour meal at El Celler de Can Roca.

Toss the Mini Boden catalog to Sara and say, "You can pick out whatever clothes you like for GR." She considered this one of the best perks of her job, even better than the four-hour meal at El Celler de Can Roca.

Many of those clothes are now put away, waiting for the day when Sara has a baby, a day that GR sees as the looming catastrophe of her life.

She's not wrong.

4.

"To con oneself into thinking that the person who provides daily physical care to a child is not the one he is going to love in a singular and primal way—a way obviously designed by nature herself to cleave child to mother and vice versa—is to ignore one of the most fundamental truths of childhood."

Essayist Caitlin Flanagan wrote those words in 2004, in an article on nannies that remains her best-known work, "How Serfdom Saved the Women's Movement." By her account, she "softened" this piece when it later appeared in her first book, but not by much. Six years later, the essay was still on my mind when I hired Sara. It is still on my mind.

Flanagan is a professional provocateur who says outrageous things in a witty enough way that she's seldom asked to be consistent. She's comfortable with sweeping statements that rely on anecdotes drawn from her own narrow world. For example, she asserts there are only two types of nanny-mother relationships—one in which a woman and nanny see each other for only minutes, at either end of the day, and one in which "mother and nanny work side by side . . . relationships of exquisite intensity." (My relationship with Sara did not fit into either of these models.) Flanagan compares the mother-nanny dynamic to the mistress-maid relationships in slavery, adding, "One does not want to compare oneself to a slaveholder." Except—she just did.

She tut-tut-tuts about professional women who consider themselves oppressed when they are the oppressors, then admits she had no idea she should pay Social Security taxes for her nanny, a Honduran woman named Paloma, whom she adored. ("She used to weigh 116 pounds! It makes us laugh to think of it. But I've seen the photographs; it's true." What a fun way to bond with your employer.) The piece centers on Flanagan's realization that it is wrong—illegal and immoral—not to pay Social Security tax for one's employees. She tries to be arch about her heroic journey to do the right thing, but ultimately she seems really impressed by her decision to follow the law. Then her twin boys became verbal and she realized, "I wasn't ill-suited to the vocation; I just wasn't much of a baby person." Bye-bye, Paloma.

Flanagan's current bio at the *Atlantic* says she "lives in California, where she spends her time writing and raising twins." Given that the twins should be midway through college by now, I am curious how she's "raising" them, but I guess a mother's job is never done. Even when it's contracted out.

I have the resources to live the Flanagan ideal—
mother at home, father bringing home the big television
bucks. (Her husband makes Barbie movies.) Although I
make pretty good coin for a novelist, my husband's success as a television producer dwarfs mine. He earns ten
times what I do. He has ten times as many Twitter follow-
ers, too, a correlation I find amusing, as if there is a secret quantitative formula somewhere that determines our
worth. He would probably argue that he has ten times as
many headaches, ten times as many problems, ten times
as many people pulling on him, demanding his attention,
and reminding him of deadlines. I don't disagree.

If I hadn't continued to write after my daughter was
born, our household would not have missed my income
and the world of literature would have gone on, as it always does. I could have abandoned myself to full-time
motherhood if I chose. I did not choose. And I have never
had a single pang of guilt about this. In the early years, I
often sat at a tiny desk inches from the kitchen table and
wrote while Sara prepared my daughter's breakfast. By
Flanagan's calculation, love that should have been mine
was transferred instead to the woman my daughter still
calls "Yaya."

To which I say: So what? My daughter's love, best I can tell, is an enormous resource. Not infinite, but capacious and varied. Her love for me is different from her love for my husband. Not deeper or more profound, just different. Her love for Yaya is singular, beautiful, and complex. She tries to articulate it. "I don't love Yaya more than you," she says. "Well, maybe a little more. But, really, I just love her in a different way. She might be number one, but you're really close. It's sort of a tie. But if I had to put someone number one, it would probably be Yaya."

This is after five years in which I have shouldered most of her daily care, although between school and after-school programs and a part-time babysitter (who's really my assistant), I have managed to protect my forty-hour workweek. I cook dinner at least four weeknights out of five, adhering to themes my daughter has established (for example, "Tenderloin Tuesday," "Breakfast for Dinner," "Around-the-World Thursday"). I make beds, I change the sheets, I even fold the fitted sheets, using a technique I learned on YouTube. I send in homemade cookies for school bake sales. I try to chaperone at least one field trip a year.

I have gone from being a complete incompetent as a

parent to believing myself an excellent mother, a transition that would have been impossible if Yaya was still with us.

That said, I'd have her back in a heartbeat, renounce all my new skills—maybe not the folded fitted sheets and homemade cookies, I'm smug about those—because I have no problem conceding that Sara is a superior caretaker to me in every way. When Sara's with GR, she's never in a hurry to get anywhere because she's already where she is supposed to be. She is in the moment and in the role she has chosen. Whereas I am always feeling the push-and-pull of my other work.

Yes, I just described being a parent as work. Amazing how subversive that sounds, two decades into the twenty-first century. For all the ways we try to tailor our language—dropping the phrase "working mother" and speaking of those who "work *outside* the home"—we're still a little squeamish about the fact that child-rearing is a job and a lot of us outsource it. Instead of judging a culture that makes this difficult and expensive, we judge each other. There is literally no choice that a woman can make that someone won't denounce. Flanagan derided upper-middle-class women's reliance on immigrants; I took a swipe at Flanagan's indifference to labor laws. I know some people wondered why I didn't stay at home during my child's early years. Conversely, others suggested I should have even more help.

No one is more critical of the decisions I make than my daughter, who keeps probing my psyche with her sticky little fingers, trying to find the hot-white center of my guilt. To hear my daughter tell it, no one's mother works more than hers. I point to the log at the after-care program, which documents which kids get picked up at four forty-five, as she does, and which ones have to stay until six-thirty. I take advantage of my flexible schedule to show up for almost every school event. But the facts don't matter. She doesn't believe I put her first, whereas she never doubted that she was all that mattered to Yaya.

5.

In every nanny story, it's a given that the nanny leaves. Mary Poppins leaves. Ole Golly leaves. Mrs. Doubtfire is unmasked, literally.

It's also a given that those left behind are wiser, better people. Harriet the Spy adjusts to life without Ole Golly.

Mr. Banks learns to have fun, at least in the Disney film. Neither the book nor the film is much interested in Mrs. Banks. The movie only created the suffragette business for her because no one could imagine what she did all day when she had a retinue of servants.

One last given: The nanny story is never about the nanny. Even if it's one of those scary tales in which the nanny attempts to destroy the family, it's still about the mother, the implicit risk of hiring another person to do what you are supposed to be able to do by instinct. What you are supposed to yearn to do, if possible. That message is everywhere, still. Real women breastfeed. Real women, good women, given the opportunity that so few of us have now, will choose to be full-time mothers.

A woman like me, a woman who didn't give birth, a woman who could afford to be a full-time mom, should be especially vulnerable to this pressure. But I honestly never gave a shit, and not because I delude myself that my work is important. My books are entertaining, or should be, but I'm not saving the world here. I'm saving myself.

This nanny story is about the nanny, about the humility one learns from watching someone breezily excel at a job you will never master. This is a story about a twenty-four-year-old woman who blew into my life without a carpetbag, yet still had an endless supply of magical tricks. Again and again I wondered: *How did she know how to do that?* I can tell you this much: She didn't learn her techniques from a book.

The irony of the nanny story is that the nanny is paid, but the children in her care never see her affection as conditional or transactional. Nor should they.

No longer our employee, Sara is family now. We see her when we visit New Orleans or when she returns to her parents' home in Maryland. During the December holidays, our Jewish daughter goes to Yaya's, where she bakes Christmas cookies and gets an early visit from Santa. ("How did he know exactly what I wanted?" she marvels every year.) When Sara married in September 2018, our daughter was her flower girl. Her dress cost more than anything I've ever worn, and I've attended the Emmys twice. But Yaya, in true Yaya fashion, delivered what so many brides promise and rarely provide: a wedding that was more of a party, and a good one, at that.

Still, our daughter broods. She loves Yaya. But their relationship is changing, as relationships inevitably do. What will happen if Yaya has a baby? Will GR still be her #1? Can she help Yaya care for her baby? I assure her that everything will be fine, even as I inspect all those beautiful Mini Boden dresses for moth holes and hope they will one day be worn again. Yaya, on top of everything else, has good taste.

We don't get to choose our luck. I wasn't so lucky in the newspaper business, I've been incredibly lucky in publishing. I was unlucky in marriage #1, lucky in marriage #2.

But my greatest luck, my best luck, was stumbling on Sara. Maybe my daughter does love her more than she loves me. Maybe love is like a mutual fund, in which different stocks wax and wane over a lifetime. I'm confident in my value; I know I'm a blue chip and that my daughter's portfolio is diverse, as it should be. I'll be the plodding, unexciting IBM alongside Sara's Disney stock.

We all want the best for our children. In hiring Yaya and getting the hell out of her way, I gave my daughter exactly that.

My Brilliant Friend

1987

The 1980s is a punching-bag decade and it deserves this fate. One of the era's most cherished storytellers, director John Hughes, kept foisting assholes on us and insisting they were great guys. Yeah, no. Ferris Bueller is a dick, John Bender in *The Breakfast Club* is a dick, the Geek rapes an unconscious girl—with her boyfriend's consent, so add dreamboat Jake Ryan of *Sixteen Candles* to the John Hughes dick parade. Look, I think Kevin in *Home Alone* is kind of dickish.

But the 1980s aligned more or less with my twenties and I believe one is honor-bound to have affection for the bad hair, bad clothes, bad music, and bad choices of one's youth. I had a perm. I wore bejeweled bolos with oversized shirts, riotous Adrienne Vittadini sweaters, Willie Smith dresses, white oxfords with little lace socks. I regret nothing. Okay, maybe the bolos.

My twenties were spent in Texas, first Waco and then San Antonio. I was a reporter who liked but didn't love reporting. I wanted to write fiction and lord knows I tried. I wrote a series of short stories about an assessor-collector from Waco, Texas, who has complicated feelings about his new sister-in-law from Baltimore. I started novel after novel about a tall young woman who worked as a reporter and made poor choices in love. To call my work autobiographical is kind; it represented a total failure of imagination.

Waco was a challenging place to have fun. San Antonio, however, was perfect for a twenty-something whose fashion icon was Rosanne Cash in the "I Don't Know Why You Don't Want Me" video. On Friday and Saturday nights, my friends and I would go to clubs to dance—Los Padrinos, the Beauregard, St. Mary's Bar and Grill. Sunday mornings were for big Tex-Mex breakfasts, then, if it was hot—and it was hot eight months out of the year—tubing trips down the Guadalupe River, our inner tubes roped together, a cooler of beer riding in the one fitted with a plywood bottom.

My favorite weekend ritual was a solitary one: On Saturday morning, I rose before eight A.M. and cleaned my funky duplex while listening to *Weekend Edition* with Scott Simon. I then went to a beloved café, Twin Sisters, where I drank coffee and ate what was called, without irony or explanation, "Jewish coffeecake." At ten A.M., I sloshed out of the café and crossed the street to the Bookstop, a Texas chain that no longer exists. I bought whatever my heart desired. My heart desired trade paperback originals, an innovation in publishing popularized by the success of Jay McInerney's *Bright Lights, Big City*. Almost every major publisher had introduced a trade paperback line, usually a mix of debut writers and the backlists of writers who hadn't found the traction they deserved.

The summer of 1987 saw the start of Bantam's New Fiction line. Two debut novels, Glenn Savan's *White Palace* and Ann Hood's *Somewhere Off the Coast of Maine,* were its first releases. In reviewing Savan's novel (favorably) for the *Los Angeles Times*, critic Tom Jenks first provided the context of this new wave in publishing: "Store windows, aisles, counters were given over to inexpensive soft covers

so handsome, so pliable that anyone wants to touch them—
the packagers' successful sense of *objet*—heightened colors, strong graphics, the urban aura of money and cocaine,
sex, ennui, despair, knockoffs of chilly modern art, MTV,
record album covers, slick surfaces." Young writers were
being discovered everywhere—in New York's club scene,
in Joe McGuinniss's class at Bennington, in the pages of
Spy magazine. But no one was discovering *me*.

Savan's book provoked some mild envy, but Hood's
made me *insane*. More than thirty years later, I can still
see myself in my San Antonio bedroom, the only air-
conditioned room in my duplex. The bedroom's nine—
nine!—windows had dusty rose paper blinds from Pier
One, a small pink-and-green rug, and an antique oak
bed that I would lose in a divorce fifteen years later.

I lay across that bed, miserable, staring at the author's
photo on the back of *Somewhere Off the Coast of Maine*.
She was not quite thirty. She had no connections—no famous family, no Ivy League institution. Her bio said she
was a flight attendant who had attended the University of
Rhode Island and New York University. And—shit, shit,
shit—she was beautiful and slender, with this amazing
blond mane. Excuse the cliché, but there was no other

word for Ann Hood's hair. It was a mane, thick and full. I think I cried in my envy and fury. It felt as if someone had stolen my life, the one I was sure I deserved.

Reader, I married her.

2000

"Won't you be my number two?" Joe Jackson sang in 1984. It was a love song of sorts, asking a woman if she was up for taking care of a man who had lost his number one. It will be easy, the man assures her, because there's not much left of him. Who would sign on for such a fate?

I did, throughout my twenties and into my thirties. Over and over and over again. I remember their names still, the number ones who had broken the hearts of the men who allowed me to be their number two. I remember their stories—the one who married a daring journalist, the one who had been married to my boyfriend's best friend and was therefore forever off-limits, the one who was engaged to two men at once.

I also was the number two friend, Audrey Meadows to several Doris Days. My crushes inevitably gravitated to the beautiful, charismatic women whose company I kept. The bartender at Los Padrinos. The young French-man in my Spanish class. A colleague here or there. In the movie in my head, I was the lead—who isn't? But in life, I was not, I am not. I've never even managed to be someone's first wife.

You get used to it, being a perennial number two. It even has its advantages. As a mother, I have my share of flaws and missteps, but my daughter will never have to worry that I'll try to do a Snow White on her. I like my face. Well, that's not true. I *love* my face. It is lopsided and round, with an upturned nose that annoys professional photographers assigned to take portraits of me. "Lower your chin. Lower, lower, lower—too low. A little up. Too high! A little down." No, I'm quite clear that I've never been the fairest of them all, but still—what a *punim*! I'd squeeze my own cheeks if I could.

Ann Hood's first author photo was taken by Jerry Bauer, a photographer who had a predilection for mak-ing women prop their chins on their fists. She's wearing a black blouse and an expensive-looking white coat. I know now that she hates the photo. The coat was bor-rowed from a friend, she never intended to wear it for her portrait, but Bauer insisted on shooting outside because he liked the light. When she looks at the photo, all she can see is that coat, which is phony and inauthentic, something she never would have owned even if she could have afforded it.

Thirteen years after making myself miserable staring at Ann Hood's author photo, I met Jerry Bauer at the Baltimore train station. He had been hired by my UK publisher to take the author photo for my fifth book, my first to be published in that territory. It also was my first hardcover publication in the United States. I had started as a paperback writer, too, but as a mass-market writer with Avon Books. This was the opposite of cool. My covers were not pliable; no one yearned to touch them. One of my best friends told me her book club wouldn't even consider mass-market paperbacks—too down-market. But, finally, I was going to publish in a format that my friend's book club might consider. Assuming they read genre fiction.

"The light's good here," Bauer said, and quickly took several black-and-white shots of me. Chin down, he said. *Down, down, down—not that far down!* I don't think we ever left the train station.

The resulting photo was flattering. I look happy. I was

not. I was in the final days of a terrible flu, weak and shaky. No one else in Baltimore had this flu in the spring of 2000. It felt like a punishment for leaving my first husband, who had not done any of the things that make it easy to explain why a marriage must end. Still, I was determined to divorce him.

After fleeing my husband and my house with nothing but a suitcase and a laptop, I lived in a small apartment my parents used for Baltimore's winter months. They did not have cable television, so I sat on their bed at night and watched whatever the major broadcast networks had on tap, drinking wine, despite my therapist's advice that I avoid alcohol during this transition. In my memory, the TV was black-and-white, but that seems unlikely even for my parsimonious parents. However, I am confident in my recollection that network television in 2000 was god-awful.

A new show called *Survivor* premiered on May 31, 2000, and was an instant hit. My editors at the *Baltimore Sun* forced me to write about it, which made me grumpy. I didn't want to write about *Survivor*. I was living *Survivor*, less than a mile from my house, the one I bought before my marriage, the one filled with *my* furniture and *my* art and *my* Fiestaware, collected at Texas flea markets in the 1980s. I had published four novels, but what had it gotten me? A few awards, but almost no attention and certainly not a living wage.

I was about to have the worst year of my life to date.

Ann Hood was still a stranger to me, living the life that I thought I wanted—writing, teaching, and traveling, the mother of two children. Ann Hood had published nine books, a mix of fiction, nonfiction, and memoir. No one made Ann Hood write about *Survivor*. Ann Hood won important awards for her work. I won awards that matter in crime fiction, awards of which I was proud, but their names were silly. Edgar, Anthony, Agatha, Shamus—my awards sounded like the siblings in an E. Nesbit novel.

Two years after my bad year, Ann Hood would suffer one of the single worst tragedies the world has on offer. For a while, she wouldn't write at all. But I never noticed that this prolific writer had stopped producing new work. I could see only myself. What I wanted, what I'd accomplished, how life was punishing me. Where I stood relative to others. Was I more successful, less successful?

I was such an asshole.

2007

I remember a declaration of love, a hearty laugh. It was January 2007 and Ann Hood was the guest lecturer in the program where I was a worker bee, Eckerd College's Writers in Paradise. The workshop was only three years old and I was in my second year as a teacher. I had been recruited by the program's cofounder, Dennis Lehane, whom I had known for more than a decade. When he approached me to join the faculty, I demurred, pointing out that I had no advanced degree. I had taught creative writing only twice, as an adjunct.

"Laura," he said, "we're just looking to hire people who aren't assholes."

So that was the credential on which I was hired. I was not an asshole. According to Dennis.

An Eckerd alum, Dennis was intent on making the workshop one of the best in the country. He wooed his famous friends to make appearances—Stephen King, Richard Price, and now Ann Hood. Ann and I were in a car together, being driven to campus by one of Ann's former students. He had to introduce her and he told Ann, in passing, that he had always been a little bit in love with her. A joke of sorts, but it was my inference that he would not mind if his joke were taken seriously.

Ann threw back her head and laughed. Not in a mean way. Ann's laugh is full-bodied and rich, a generous laugh, always on tap. We arrived at campus and she bounded from the car. (Her admirer offered to help me from the backseat, extending a hand as if I were a frail grandmother. I was two weeks shy of my forty-eighth birthday, two years younger than Ann.) Within minutes, after an effusive introduction in which her former student made it clear that he was gaga for her, Ann took the stage and read from her new novel, *The Knitting Circle*. It centers on a woman who has lost her young daughter, suddenly and terribly. The woman is so paralyzed by grief that she can barely function. Knitting is her only distraction.

It was Ann's story, fictionalized. A year later, she published a memoir, *Comfort*, about what happened to her and her family in April 2002. Her daughter had strep, Ann took her to the hospital. She watched her die. "Are you writing this down?" people kept asking, as if writing were a cure.

I have read *The Knitting Circle* and *Comfort*. I have

heard Ann read from them. I know that Grace's death was not the first unexpected tragedy of her life; her brother died in his twenties. Her father died before she was fifty. She is divorced from the father of her children—Sam, Grace, and Annabelle, adopted from China five years after Grace's death.

But when I think about Ann, the first word that comes to mind is fun. Ann is always fun. She loves good food and good drink. She likes games of all stripes. She travels constantly. She tells rollicking stories on herself—the time a gorilla in Uganda tried to choose her as his mate, the time she didn't wear underwear to her daughter's first-grade graduation party and ended up falling and striking her head, so she was carried out on a stretcher and all she could think about was her lack of underwear. A story about an adventure on Block Island, known by its punch line: "Don't let the blind one drive!"

After Ann's guest-star stint at Eckerd in 2007, she joined the faculty, returning every year. The faculty live in the same bed-and-breakfast, travel in the same van. In the safe space of the van, we gossip about our students, share the occasional nightmare of a manuscript. We talk about the email we get from the world at large. One time,

I was going on and on about an inappropriate email, one in which a reader decided to tell me her life story before launching into a diatribe about my work.

Ann offered quietly, without self-pity or challenge, "My email tends to be pretty depressing." It took me a beat, but I got it. People write Ann about death and illness and personal tragedy. Her memoir-writing classes are filled with students trying to tell heartbreaking stories in the hope that they will make sense of them. Ann could be a modern-day Miss Lonelyhearts and no one would blame her.

Instead, Ann is the friend who likes to make sure we have plenty of wine and snacks wherever we are, the one who texts me every time a new Stephen Sondheim production is announced in New York. Ann likes to watch *Top Chef*, which is my kind of reality show. (I don't want to watch people eating bugs, I want to watch people eating amazing hors d'oeuvres made with gas station vending machine items.)

Heck, Ann married a top chef, Michael Ruhlman, a writer who has collaborated with famous chefs on their cookbooks, while also producing his own signature works.

Reader, to clarify, when I said I married her, I meant I officiated.

2017

We had been drinking after a long day at a New England book festival when I blurted out that I should marry Ann and Michael. I am embarrassed by this now—I really didn't have the standing to volunteer for such an intimate job. They seemed a little startled, appropriately so, by my gin-inspired bravado. They said they would think about it.

A few weeks later, they circled back to me and said, yes, why not. I took my officiating duties seriously. My second marriage had been performed by John Waters, and the man who calls himself the Pope of Trash had been touchingly earnest in our brief ceremony, attended only by my husband's son, thirteen at the time.

Ann Hood's wedding was, inevitably, a literary wedding. The readings included Robert Frost, Raymond Carver, Emily Dickinson, Donald Hall, a portion of *The Velveteen Rabbit*, Charlie Simic's "Crazy About Her Shrimp." How Ann's mother, Gogo, grimaced at the word "tits" in that poem. In less than a year, she would be gone.

As the officiant, I closed the ceremony with a reading from a Laurie Colwin short story. Colwin is an important writer to Ann, Michael, and me. There's no one quite like her. She wrote stories and novels about people you would like to be; she gave her characters room to make bad mistakes—and recover from them. She cared about food, too; her recipe for roast chicken might be better known than her fiction. Ann, inspired by Colwin's recipe for tomato pie, wrote a piece that was chosen for *The Best American Food Writing*, an achievement of which I am openly envious, despite never having written about food.

"Passion and Affect," the story from which I read, was eventually expanded to a novel, but Colwin omitted the passage that I love best. In it, two couples celebrate one's recent wedding. The bride, Misty Berkowitz, realizes that "affection and love were general, once they had been specified." In love with her new husband, she loves everything she sees, everything she can imagine—friends, furniture, telephone operators. They toast to a "deeply wonderful life."

Colwin died in the fall of 1992 at the age of forty-eight. I read her obituary while working the daytime cop shift at the *Baltimore Sun*. Within a week, the man who was to become my first husband would injure his back and I had this fleeting thought while running up and down the stairs with trays of food: *You will forever be taking care of him*. I shouted the thought down and married him anyway. We lasted less than eight years.

In 2003, Glenn Savan, author of *White Palace*, the book that was published alongside Ann Hood's, died at the age of forty-nine. He had written only one more novel and his obituary revealed that he had Parkinson's. In Providence, Rhode Island, Ann Hood could not write at all. It was the first-year anniversary of Grace's death.

That same year, I published a book I hoped would change my life. It did and it didn't. Reviews were positive, but not effusive. There's a reason they call it damning with faint praise. One review in particular broke my heart. I lay down on the floor of my laundry room, curled into the fetal position, and sobbed.

God, I was an asshole.

2019

I am writing this in a farmhouse in Tuscany. I am here because of Ann Hood. Almost a decade ago, she discovered Spannocchia, a 110-acre farm now devoted to tourism. Here, Ann has created what I like to call a destination writers' workshop. Students travel from the U.S. to study with her and other writers. Since 2015, I have been lucky enough to be one of the teachers. This year feels like Eckerd-Euro; the other instructors are Andre Dubus III and Stewart O'Nan, also regulars in the Eckerd workshop. We have been joined by an assortment of spouses and offspring.

How do writers learn to live without envy? We tell our students that it's not a finite-sum game, that there is enough success to go around, enough shelf space for all the good books. With digitization, this is at once truer than ever and falser, too. Yes, everything can be published. You can sit at your laptop and upload your novel with the push of a single button. But who will find it, who will read it?

Stories about writers tend toward rivalries, whether it's Martin Amis's *The Information* or the silly old movie *Rich and Famous*. Every writer knows the wonderful poem, penned by Clive James, "The Book of My Enemy Has Been Remaindered." We are encouraged to accept false binaries—one can have artistic *or* financial success, never both. If one friend is up, the other must be down.

I have ended up having a lovely career, something I am reluctant to state so flatly for fear it will be taken from me. Yet there are still things I yearn for, shiny objects of prestige on my friends' shelves, literally and figuratively. This fellowship, that teaching gig, this award, that milestone. To quote Veruca Salt, that wonderful role model: I want the works.

I know good writers who have failed at this gig and mediocre writers who have succeeded. I know bad people who have conned the world into believing they are humble and helpful. I know even more good people who receive no credit—who seek no credit—for their acts of kindness to other writers. In short: Writers, like Soylent Green, are people.

I look back across three-plus decades and see myself in my San Antonio bedroom reading Ann Hood's first novel. Those nine windows—nine!—in dusty rose paper shades that have almost certainly decomposed in some landfill by now. The pretty pink-and-green rug, long gone. All the furniture, ditto. Not just the bed, but a quilt box, a pine night table, an Art Deco wardrobe. The outrageous 1980s clothes are gone, too; I miss those most of all. Okay, maybe not the bolos.

That young woman is gone. Her, I don't miss. She is petty and envious. She'd make a good secondary character in a John Hughes movie, one of the "yes" girls who surround the Queen Bee. Her imagination is limited, a terrible thing in a writer. She cannot begin to see where her life will take her, can never imagine herself thirty-two years in the future, writing these words while sitting at a marble-topped kitchen table in an Italian farmhouse. Why is her imagination so stunted when it comes to her own life? Why is she willing to settle for so little? Why does she want so much?

If I could go back in time and tell her that it will be all right, that her future will outstrip her dreams—I wouldn't. She doesn't deserve this information. I don't want to share with her what I have learned. I condemn her to do everything I have done, even the mistakes, especially the mistakes. I'd throw in some more mistakes if I could. The only thing I would deign to tell her is how puny her pain is. Envying other writers, crying over a review—if this is what the bad fairy brings to your christening, consider yourself lucky. Don't you understand that you are going to know real pain?

Worse, you are going to cause it.

Here in Tuscany, it's almost five P.M., cocktail hour. We are having Aperol spritzes served in Mason jars, the only broad-bottomed glasses available in the local grocery store, with ice cubes made in leftover egg cartons, as we don't have ice trays. We are pathetically proud of this innovation, our Instagram-worthy Mason jars of spritzes, our egg-carton ice cubes. We will stand on the terrace, the writers and the brave people who love us, and drink to a deeply wonderful life.

Men Explain *The Wire* to Me[1]

In July 1999, Apple began selling a series of laptops in bright, trippy colors. The iBook was also referred to as the clamshell; shut, it had a nifty little handle that allowed you to carry it without a case, reminiscent of a purse Wilma might use on *The Flintstones*. It came in orange and blue and, a few months later, lime-green.

The iBook would be sold for only nineteen months, although there are still some enthusiasts who use refurbished versions. I bought an orange one in the fall of 1999

---

1 This title was inspired by an incident on Facebook in which I jokingly wondered at the answer to a *New York Times* crossword puzzle clue, "a character on *The Wire*," and a man earnestly explained to me that it was Omar, then proceeded to tell me about the show.

and it served me for four years, dying a dignified death in 2003. Today, it sits in a small, incomplete graveyard of my former computers, sharing the top of a credenza with a bright blue iMac and the MacIntosh Classic II on which I wrote my first three novels.

But it is the clamshell that will be of particular interest to archivists, I think, because it contains not only every version of my sixth, seventh, and eighth novels, but also a scrap of a teleplay, in which a police officer named Jimmy McArdle puzzles over the death of a guy named Snot Boogie, whose bad habit of stealing the pot from a regular street-corner crap game has finally gotten him killed. Why, McArdle asks a witness, was Snot Boogie allowed to join the game time and time again if he always stole the money?

Got to, the witness said. *This is America.*

I can feel the fanboys in the crowd stirring and jostling, eager to jump to the punch line: It was the pilot for *The Wire*! McArdle's name was changed to McNulty because no one at HBO liked McArdle! Executive producer Bob Colesberry suggested the new surname!

Good fanboys. Sit down, fanboys. You may know more

about *The Wire* than I do; as much as I love and admire the show created by the man who is now my husband, I doubt I could win a pub quiz devoted to the topic. But you do not know *this* story about *The Wire*, a story only I can tell, and you must let me have the floor.

This is America.

Development

Where does anything begin? I always want to attribute that line to Stephen Sondheim, but he wrote, in *A Little Night Music*, *Doesn't anything begin*, which is quite different.

The Wire began in the large-ish head of David Judah Simon, born in 1960 in a Washington, D.C., hospital. I'm not being rude about his head; it is slightly larger than normal, although not as freakishly large as I supposed it to be when I bought him a gorgeous Borsalino wool baseball cap in Rome, a hat that fits no one. This hat would swim on Charlie Brown's head.

Lots of words have been amassed in profiles of David. I'm not here to write another one because (a) there

have been plenty,[2] and (b) ick. But I do think one person
has been criminally neglected in any discussion of David
and his work, and that person is—his mother, Dorothy
Simon. David was her youngest child by a bit; brother
Gary was thirteen, sister Linda was ten when David was
born. Family lore has it that David was conceived the
night of Gary's bar mitzvah, and the math adds up. Anyway, by the time David arrived, Dorothy had decided
that all children needed in order to flourish was love.[3]

So she didn't worry when she found David lying curled
up in the clothes dryer one day, trying to figure out how
it worked. She didn't worry when a police officer—Well,
those stories are David's to tell. All you need to know is
that he grew up relatively unencumbered and uncowed
by authority.

He also had remarkable self-confidence. But then, all of

---

2 These include a twelve-thousand-word piece in the *New Yorker*, a
   six-thousand-word piece in the *New York Times Magazine,* and, perhaps most infamously, an *Atlantic* piece that called him "The Angri-
   est Man in Television."

3 My favorite story about my mother-in-law centers on our first meeting. It was at the premiere for *The Corner*; David and I had just
   started dating. I introduced myself and she said, "I'm looking for
   my other son. Not famous, but a doctor."

the Simon siblings were successful. Linda, who died at the age of thirty-nine, was an outstanding artist whose work was once included in a show at the Baltimore Museum of Art. Gary is a specialist in infectious diseases and has an endowed chair at George Washington University.

Anyway, to simplify: David Simon was born into a loving family in which he was encouraged to follow his dreams. By the time I met him, thirty years later, he seemed disgustingly successful to me.

He was just getting started.

The Bit Player

There's a moment in the film *Shakespeare in Love* that I'm told is inspired by an old theatrical joke. The actor who plays the nurse is asked in the pub what this new play, *Romeo and Juliet*, is about. "It's about this nurse," the actor begins.

Consider this the "it's-about-this-nurse" portion of our program, in which the onlooker puts herself front and center in a story in which she is actually peripheral to the action. But I just want to explain how I happened on my bird's-eye view of *The Wire*.

As a young journalist, all I wanted to do was get back to Baltimore, my hometown. You would think that having a father at the newspaper would be helpful. You would be wrong.

For eight years, I kept orbiting *The Sun*, as it was then known and as I prefer to call it.[4] First I was told they almost never hired anyone straight out of college. Then I was told I would need at least five years' experience. When I hit that milestone, I was informed I simply wasn't good enough.

"We need writers who can make the simplest stories sing, whose style elevates what they cover," the metro editor told me.

I was standing in the dining room of my charming dump of a duplex in San Antonio, willing myself not to cry. It's hard being told your dream job is out of reach because you suck. Years earlier, my father had told my sister never to admit fault in a car accident, but he hadn't

---

4   The nomenclature of the newspaper business founded by A. S. Abell is extremely complicated. For most of its history, the morning paper was *The Sun* and the afternoon paper was the *Evening Sun*; together they were known as the Sunpapers. Its current out-of-town corporate owner has changed the official name, but I refuse to use it.

told her what to say instead. She got into a minor fender bender and leaped from the car, shouting to the other driver: "It's all your fault!" This blunt assessment of my abilities felt like a car collision. Hurt and confused, I came out swinging.

"That's interesting," I said. "Because I read *The Sun* all the time and I don't think most of your writers fit that description."

"That's why we need to hire some," the editor said.

The Sun was a serious newspaper that took itself very seriously. Big Washington bureau, foreign bureaus. Its sister paper, the *Evening Sun*, was more rambunctious, Costello to *The Sun*'s Abbott. In August 1989, five people gave notice in a single week. A friend on staff gave me what turned out to be a winning strategy: Find a way to get to Baltimore on my own dime, then call the editors and say I just happened to be in town. It was my decision not to mention that my father was an award-winning editorial writer and columnist on the morning paper. The editors figured it out; they were newsmen, after all. But it only made them like me better. I was hired to cover social services, a broad beat that encompassed poverty, homelessness, juvenile justice, and welfare programs. It was the best gig I had in twenty years of journalism.

David Simon was on book leave when I arrived. The first time I heard his name, it was when one reporter asked another when "Simon" would return, then commented on what an amazing writer he was. I immediately took against him. It was galling to me that he had been one of the rare reporters *The Sun* had hired straight from college, that he had a book deal when he wasn't quite thirty. Then the book, *Homicide: A Year on the Killing Streets*, was optioned for television by Barry Levinson, at the time Baltimore's foremost chronicler.[5]

By 1991, the year David's book was published, the staffs of the two papers had merged and *Evening Sun* reporters had to sit among our former competitors. In *The Sun's* newsroom in the 1990s, reporters shared computers, big hulking systems called Coyotes. The Coyotes sat on turn-

---

5 Who is Baltimore's foremost chronicler? The names mentioned most often now are David, Anne Tyler, and John Waters. But David has yet to return to Baltimore in his subsequent television productions and Tyler's work isn't really concerned with the city, it's just set here. So I'd vote for John Waters.

tables that could be rotated between two desks. If your deskmate was on deadline, you had to find someplace else to work.

One morning, I arrived to find that my desk-size calendar blotter had been used to, well, blot what appeared to be gallons of coffee. It was damp, beginning to ripple. Outraged, I set out to learn who had used my desk the night before. "Simon," another reporter told me. "Simon was at your desk last night."

I tracked him down to yell at him. He apologized and asked how he could make it right. I told him he could give me a signed copy of his book. He signed on the title page: "Do you want cream with that, Hon?"[6]

And that was the beginning of—nothing. He was married. I was engaged. He was morning *Sun* and I was *Evening Sun*. He was royalty and I was a peasant. About the same time, yet another *Sun* editor told me the reason I got stuck with dud assignments was because I wasn't a very good writer. I realized that as long as this man was my boss, I was going to have a hard

---

6   Yes, we still have this copy.

time changing his mind. But if I wrote a novel, then the verdict on my talent would be decided by a much larger jury.[7]

Fast-forward five years: I published my second novel, a mass-market paperback original called *Charm City*. About the same time, my now-former colleague David Simon published his second work of nonfiction, *The Corner*.[8] One day, I met David at a radio station for an appearance; we then had several hours of downtime before a bookstore signing at a mall.

David suggested we go to a diner. We didn't know each other well. Over a late breakfast at the Double T Diner, he told me his idea for a novel. Not a crime novel, more of a black comedy, in which a frustrated cop manages to create a fake crisis, in which it appears a serial killer is preying on the city's homeless. He wanted to know if the plot sounded credible to me.

---

7 The editor was Gil Watson and I rather liked him. I definitely admired him for his directness, quite different from some other editors I had at *The Sun*.

8 David took a buyout from the paper in 1995 and went to work on the staff of the television show based on his first book. My father, as it happens, took the same buyout.

Yes, you *Wire* fanboy, the one in the back, the one in the flannel shirt with a man bun. No, the one in the *blue* flannel shirt. Yes, yes, yes, the plot of the never-written novel was almost identical to the fifth and most reviled season of *The Wire*.

Bonus points if you know that I appeared as an extra, a reporter named Laura Lippman, who had one line to say. I was singled out in some reviews as being emblematic of everything that was wrong with Season 5 of *The Wire*.

But I'm getting ahead of myself.

Season One

David was out of work when we began dating during the summer of 2000. I always like to state that for the record because people who don't know our history tend to type me as a gold digger. I assumed he would work again, but he was living off his savings, trying to figure out what to do next.

Homicide, the NBC television show based on his book, had gone off the air in 1999. The same year, David made a miniseries based on his second book, *The Corner*. But even after winning two Emmys for *The Corner* in September 2000, he hadn't found a new gig.[9]

Oh, he had lots of job possibilities, but they were all in Los Angeles and he had a young son he was co-parenting with his ex in Maryland. He shopped a screenplay co-written with the *Washington Post*'s Gene Weingarten called *Pie the Man*.[10] This led to a script assignment from Ron Howard, who was interested in making a film based on the true story of some guys from Scranton who attempted to break the Guinness world record for consecutive piano-playing. That bought him some time.

In the summer of 2001, the question of employment circled around again. We were on vacation with two other families in the Outer Banks when David's agent

---

9   In Los Angeles for my book tour, I attended the ceremony with him, but spent most of my time bracketed by two seat-fillers. I remember that one of David's competitors in the category for Best Mini-Series, John Stamos, was across the aisle from us with Rebecca Romijn. Cheerfuly starstruck, I turned to David and said, "You may win the Emmy over him, but he wins best date."

10   *Pie the Man* centers on four average guys from Detroit who decide that they want to throw a pie in the face of the President of the United States. After 9/11, it was deemed impossible to consider, but I think its time may have come again.

called and told him that something had fallen off HBO's schedule. If he acted quickly, he might be able to launch "that cop show you're always talking about."

We were in the car when the call came, driving five rambunctious boys to a community swimming pool. We dropped them off and circled back to the house, where I gave David my laptop. I didn't have a screenwriting program, so he worked in a Microsoft Word document.

Of course, within a few days he was back on his own computer, using proper screenwriting software. I don't remember much of the summer of 2001—I was distracted by my job woes and the official dissolution of my marriage, which, per Maryland law, was taking more than two years. Then 9/11 came, followed by days when *everything* seemed uncertain, not just the future of a television pilot. By December, when David went to New York to oversee the pilot's editing and final mix, I had left the newspaper and submitted my seventh novel. I was going to be a full-time novelist. It was a giddy, amazing time.

David and his fellow executive producer, Bob Colesberry, screened the pilot for me. I loved it, of course. I couldn't wait to see more. I just had one question.

"That dead guy at the end of the show—who was it?"

They looked at me as if I were enormously stupid. The dead guy obviously was the witness in the murder case, at the beginning of the episode. Who else would it be? David and Bob, talking about me as if I weren't even there, finally decided that I couldn't follow a complicated story line.[11]

SEVERAL WEEKS LATER, HBO executives gave them essentially the same note, resulting in a pretty inelegant fix. But the show was green-lit. Three months after that, David and I decided to buy a house together. We closed during the first week of Season 1's production schedule and I had to move without David's help, a harbinger of life as the partner of a showrunner. On June 2, 2002, we sat on our new sofa in our new den and watched *The Wire* on our new television set with singer-songwriter Steve Earle, who had a small part in *The Wire*, and ate take-out sushi.

That was the premiere party.

Neil Genzlinger, in the *New York Times*, wrote: "The real questions about 'The Wire,' though, involve not the

---

11 To repeat, I had just submitted my seventh crime novel.

style, but the audience's level of tolerance . . . With its unappetizing subject matter, 'The Wire' may find it hard to compete with a moonlit summer evening."

I'm not sure what was more irksome—the mixed review or the fact that the show wasn't deemed worthy of the *Times*' first-string critic. Oh well, Matt Roush at *TV Guide* liked it.[12]

Season 2

The parties got bigger. The reviews became ecstatic. I remember sitting on the train from New York to Baltimore the morning after the Season 2 premiere party, watching David, Bob, and executive producer Nina Noble read the coverage. Bob looked absolutely stricken. "How are we going to top this?" Bob, I'm sad to say, didn't live long enough to find out. He died in February 2004, before Season 3 aired. The partnership between David and Bob

---

12 Overall, Season 1 for *The Wire* has an 85 percent critics' rating on Rotten Tomatoes, the lowest of all five seasons, with Seasons 3 and 4 earning perfect scores. The fifth season had a score of 95 percent, which might seem to contradict my assertion it was the most reviled, but those who disliked it *really* disliked it.

was an arranged marriage, dating back to *The Corner*, and it was an incredibly successful one. It seems terribly unfair that Bob didn't live long enough to see the full flower of its success.[13]

But while *The Wire* was on air, I don't think anyone working on it felt like it was a hit. A critical darling, yes. A cult fave, sure. But not a hit. As part of the HBO "family," we were invited to the *Sopranos* premiere one year. The episode was shown in Radio City Music Hall, and the party was on the ice rink, where a fake floor had been installed. William Styron sat behind us in the theater. That was what a hit looked like—a summer party on top of an ice rink, Pulitzer Prize winners in the audience.

There was one setting in which David was treated as if he were all four Beatles: crime writers conferences. Some of my male peers would almost bodily shove me out of the way to get to him. This was the man who had hired

---

13 I have so many Bob stories; I'll settle for two here. He cowrote "Hot Lunch," the song that Irene Cara "improvises" in *Fame*, and he was Nicole Kidman's body double in the nude swimming scene in *Billy Bathgate*.

George Pelecanos and Dennis Lehane. Surely he would want them, too.[14]

It was always understood that I would never join the writers' room. David raised the idea tentatively before Season 4. But we both quickly shot it down. Candor was essential to his operation; writers who felt comfortable arguing with the boss might have felt less comfortable saying the boss's wife had bum ideas.[15]

Also, I am the most extroverted loner you'll ever meet. I adore people. I just loathe collaboration. Over the years, more of my good friends have gone to work in writers' rooms, some of them run by my husband, and all I can say to them is: "You're a better woman than I am."

---

14 The thing that never seemed to occur to these guys who wanted to work for my husband is that he would ask me to vet them. George as well, but whenever David considers hiring a crime novelist, he asks me what I know.

15 To this date, David and I have worked on one project together, a so-called "jukebox" musical using the Pogues songbook. Our friend George Pelecanos is the third writer on the project, which has now entered its tenth year of development.

Season 3

"Showrunners" aren't new; the idea that a television show is shaped by its writing-producing staff has been around since the 1970s. An article in *Slate*, tracing the term's history, notes that *Variety* first used the term in 1992 and that the *New York Times* explained it in a 1995 profile of John Welles. But it's only recently that people have begun to identify it as a job to aspire to. F. Scott Fitzgerald's generation saw film work as a way to pay the bills; my cohort of boomer novelists tended to love the movies as much as books. Now terrific novelists like Tom Perrotta, Gillian Flynn, and Megan Abbott choose to work in television because they love the medium.

But in the early twenty-first century, the most famous showrunners were HBO's triumvirate of Davids: Chase, Milch, and Simon. In the early days of *The Wire*, my David gave a lot of interviews, intent on directing the conversation, telling people how to watch this cop show that wasn't a cop show. He compared it to novels such as *Moby-Dick*, which prompted all sorts of witticisms from me. ("Your television show is a book? What's the ISBN number?" "It's a novel for television? Isn't that kind of like a steak for vegetarians?")

Nevertheless, he won the propaganda war. Earnest, smart people began proclaiming that *The Wire* was better than most novels. Zadie Smith approached my husband at a party and told him that he was teaching novelists everywhere how to write better dialogue. Over the years, my husband was compared to Balzac, Cervantes, Tolstoy, Dickens, Edith Wharton,[16] Flaubert—the list goes on and on.

If you think that I'm going to launch the counterargument here, think again. *The Wire* is better than a novel. It should be. A single episode cost millions and required the work of more than a hundred people. No solo scribe can provide the same immersive experience as a medium that supplies its own sights and sounds.

But there is a fundamental difference between even the best television show and the worst novel. The television show moves forward of its own momentum; all you have to do is sit there and keep your eyes open, pay

---

16 Full credit to Richard Price for the comparison to Edith Wharton.

attention. A book, even a bad one, requires a lot more effort. A television show is like a car with cruise control, whereas a book is like an old-fashioned stick shift.

The Wire went off the air in 2008, the year that Obama was elected. In his second term, Obama invited my husband to the Oval Office to discuss drug policy.[17] By then, David was an official genius, a MacArthur Fellow. Now that I know the internal workings of the award, I wait every September for my phone to ring, certain that I am worthy, too.[18] Obviously, my husband can't put me forward, but I know some other MacArthur Fellows. Look, the idea that a television producer would get a MacArthur grant was once considered pretty out there. Why not a genre writer?[19]

---

17 I didn't go, although I was invited to accompany David. It is one of only two times I have declined to ride David's coattails to meet someone I admire; the other person was Philip Roth, at the end of his life. I regret not meeting Obama, a serious reader with great taste, but we had a very young child at home.

18 No, seriously, I do.

19 I was extremely happy when Kelly Link was recognized in the class of 2018.

Season 5[20]

The actor Hugh O'Brian is credited with coining the five stages of an actor's life:

Who is Hugh O'Brian?

Get me Hugh O'Brian.

Get me someone like Hugh O'Brian.

Get me a young Hugh O'Brian.

Who was Hugh O'Brian?

A cult television show follows a slightly different arc. What is *The Wire*? You have to watch *The Wire*. It's like *The Wire*! *The Wire* has jumped the shark.[21] What is *The Wire*?

When David's next series, *Treme*, premiered, I finally understood *The Wire*'s significance because so many of the reviews proclaimed it was not *The Wire*. Very few

---

20 Skipping Season 4 because almost everyone agrees it was *The Wire*'s best season and that grows so tiresome.

21 Jon Hein coined the term "jump the shark," in reference to an episode of *Happy Days*, and I mention this here just because I actually know Jon Hein and like him a lot.

audience members and critics remembered the time when *The Wire* wasn't *THE Wire*, just another Sunday HBO show that a *New York Times* critic worried might be too poky.

The Wire became a punch line, a cultural shorthand for something beloved and complex, but perhaps a little too difficult. On *Girls*, Hannah Horvath told her boyfriend she simply couldn't follow the show and was never going to watch it. On *The Howard Stern Show*, a staffer was mocked for his decision to play it at a slightly increased speed on his Xbox. The real meta-moment came when two characters on the shark-jumping *Glee*[22] talked about hate-watching *Treme* together.

The Wire and television recapping came of age about the same time. It amuses me now to recall that our household tech was so antiquated during *The Wire*'s original run that David had to go to his office after the initial broadcast to see what people were saying about it on the Internet. I can't even remember where he went

---

22 By my count, Ryan Murphy has trash-talked my husband twice in his work; now I've trash-talked him twice in this book. In case it's not clear by now, I play a really long game.

on the Internet to find those opinions. Now viewers live-tweet popular television shows, although it's rarer and rarer for people to watch things in real time.

To this day, I watch my husband's work "live" when possible, but I guess it's time for a confession. When the fifth and final season of *The Wire* aired in 2008, David was often working in London on the postproduction of *Generation Kill*, a miniseries. He had a DVD with the series finale of *The Wire*, but asked me to wait and watch it with him. I couldn't bear to wait. So I watched it ahead of time and then watched it again with him, pretending to be surprised at every development.

It was March 9, 2008, and we had come full circle, back to our den and the brown leather sofa, only without Steve Earle or sushi. I have zero memory of this. I'm sure I teared up; the final montage is quite moving. It had been more than a decade since David had told me his idea for a story about a cop who fakes a serial killer, and here it was, fully fleshed out.

It really was better than a novel.

Finale

My husband has two sayings that I've co-opted: "I never run faster than when I'm racing my best enemy," and "No one lives inside his success." The first one may not be the most flattering thing to admit about one's self, but the second is, I believe, essential to one's humanity. Can you imagine someone strutting around, conscious of their success? It makes me think of a greeting card I once bought my daughter, a picture of a giant anthropomorphized pickle who says, "I'm kind of a big dill."

I've spent almost twenty years now *Wire*-adjacent, knowledgeable about the show but unconnected to it, a happy gherkin alongside a big dill.

The oddest thing about *The Wire*'s legacy is that the first line of my husband's obit may already have been written, a verdict he will never accept and one reason he keeps pushing, pushing, pushing, working, working, working—and one reason I love him. He doesn't want to be known for a single show. He wants to be known for the body of his work, the totality of his vision.

Can I be objective about my husband's work? Honey,

you have no idea. It's silly to proclaim anything the single "greatest," but easy to say that *The Wire* is one of the best television shows ever made. Try to make an argument that it's not good, that it didn't change its own medium. Go ahead, try. But remember—if you come at the queen, you best not miss.

And so we circle back to the orange clamshell, sitting on my credenza. My papers and marginalia are already promised to the Peabody Library in Baltimore, the first institution to express interest. The clamshell contains a huge slice of my work, tens of thousands of words. It has fewer than two hundred words of *The Wire*. But *The Wire* is so much bigger than anything I will ever do. One can imagine *The Wire*'s orange sofa in the Smithsonian, or the Museum of Television and Film. What to do with the orange clamshell? Do we send it to the Peabody, or let it be a footnote[23] in whatever institution ends up with my husband's papers?

For now, the argument is moot. Turns out I didn't keep the power cord. The clamshell is closed tight, its secrets

---

23 Yes, this is why this piece has footnotes. I'm meta that way.

hidden from prying eyes until some really motivated IT guy gets his hands on it.

Anyway, thank you for coming to my TED talk on what it's like to watch someone close to you create a cultural phenomenon. And per the FAQ section on my website—no, I won't forward your emails to my husband.

Acknowledgments

Before I acknowledge all the people to whom I owe a debt of gratitude, I'd first like to explain this book's approach to naming names—I did, except when I didn't. In some cases, I was trying to protect someone's privacy. In other cases, I was avoiding shameless name-dropping. And in some places, I was cheerfully inconsistent. While I had no problem using my daughter's name in the essay "The Thirty-First Stocking," I later decided to be more careful about what I share about my kid in public.

Now, some gratitude.

Ann Hood and Sean Manning were two of the first people to lure me into writing about my own life. When I decided I wanted to try freelancing more, Taffy Brodesser-Akner was generous enough to provide contacts and expert advice in pitching. In fact, she usually pitched the pieces for me. Sari Botton was not only polite about my unprofessional pitch, she was a dream editor for the pieces that appeared in Longreads. Carrie Feron, my longtime editor at Morrow—twenty-four years and counting—was the one who suggested I write this book. Vicky Bijur, my longtime agent—twenty-four years and counting—cheerfully dealt with the tangle of rights and permissions for the seven essays that had been previously published. Carrie and Vicky are backed up by two equally remarkable women, Asanté Simons and Alexandra Franklin, respectively.

My husband and my daughter are pretty good sports about being pulled into my new world, as are most of my friends. A shout-out to all the moms at my daughter's school, but especially to Joyce Jones, who listened to me talk out some of these ideas on the drive to and from our weekly tennis lesson.

And, seriously, thank you to the communities I have found on social media, public and private. They are imperfect places, to be sure, with serious consequences for the world. But it's a rare day when I don't get one good laugh out of something online.

Credits

READ THE ENTIRE
LAURA LIPPMAN COLLECTION

THE TESS MONAGHAN SERIES

Baltimore Blues

Charm City

Butchers Hill

In Big Trouble

The Sugar House

In a Strange City

The Last Place

By a Spider's Thread

No Good Deeds

Another Thing to Fall

The Girl in the Green
Raincoat

Hush, Hush

MORE FROM LAURA LIPPMAN

Hardly Knew Her

Every Secret Thing

The Power of Three

What the Dead Know

Life Sentences

I'd Know You Anywhere

The Most Dangerous
Thing

And When She Was
Good

After I'm Gone

Wilde Lake

Sunburn

Lady in the Lake

My Life as a Villainess